THE BOOK OF QUESTIONS
Yaël, Elya, and Aely

EDMOND JABÈS

The Book
of Questions
Yaël, Elya, Aely

———

Translated from the French by
ROSMARIE WALDROP

WESLEYAN UNIVERSITY PRESS
Middletown, Connecticut

ACKNOWLEDGEMENTS:

Yaël, Elya, and Aely, Volumes IV, V, and VI of Le Livre des Questions, were originally published by Editions Gallimard, in 1967, 1969, and 1972 respectively.

Parts of this translation have appeared in Cream City Review, Denver Quarterly, Fiction, The Harvard Advocate, Imprint, Molly Bloom, Montemora, New Directions, OARS, Paper Air, Sub/Stance, The Literary Supplement (Writings), and in A Big Jewish Book, ed. J. Rothenberg (New York: Doubleday, Anchor, 1978), The Random House Book of Twentieth-Century French Poetry, ed. P. Auster (New York: Random House, 1982), Elya (Bolinas, CA: Tree Books, 1973) and The Death of God (Peterborough, England: Spectacular Diseases, 1979).

The translator gratefully acknowledges a prize from Columbia University's Translation Center, awarded in 1978 for this translation in progress.

She would also like to thank the author and, especially, Arlette Jabès for their invaluable help and suggestions.

All inquiries and permissions requests should be addressed to the Publisher, Wesleyan University Press, 110 Mt. Vernon Street, Middletown, Connecticut 06457

Distributed by Harper & Row Publishers, Keystone Industrial Park, Scranton, Pennsylvania 18512

Library of Congress Cataloging in Publication Data

Jabès, Edmond.

   The book of questions.

   Translation of: Le Livre des questions.

   I. Title.

PQ2619.A112L513   1983   848'.91407   83-6950

ISBN 0-8195-5086-8

Manufactured in the United States of America

First Edition

CONTENTS

YAËL

THE BOOK OF QUESTIONS

VOLUME IV

DEDICATION

You wonder about others: how do they appease
their desire to be All?

By sacrifice, conformity, trickery, poetry, moral-
ity, snobbery, heroism, religion, revolt, vanity,
money?

—GEORGES BATAILLE
L'expérience intérieure

Without trying to see more than a coincidence I
could not help noticing how exactly this meeting of
symbols corresponds to what I think is the deep
sense of suicide: to become at the same time *oneself* and *the other*, male and female, subject and
object, the killer and the killed—our only chance
of communion with ourselves.

—MICHEL LEIRIS
L'âge d'homme

He realizes that the idea of dying has become
part of this ignorance. And when she, in pain,
fighting with what she does not know, lets slip certain words to suggest that she is as it were deprived
of an end, that if she should die it would have to
be of *his* death, this thought seems to him part of
the game of ignorance played between word and
presence.

He speaks of it. The word does not betray
ignorance.

—MAURICE BLANCHOT
L'Attente l'Oubli

My voice is your life,
my faith your death,
for you, Yaël, for you
this book of a time
where our dreams find rest.

At the end of time there will be the immense
open book of space where the memory of worlds
and men will chisel as into stone its song of pain, of
tenderness, of love.

One day we shall know, Yaël, which part of our death we have
sacrificed to thirst.

(*We did not know. We were at the edge of knowing, at the eve of springs.*)

The light of going on became our logic.

. . . This dream: a dreadful smothering of the soul, then a lofty idea of death, then an ordinary note pad where the day butts against the night.

FORE-SPEECH

I say: I am death, and forthwith am before God was.

If we spurn God's image, do we not reject creation?

Then where is truth but in the burning space between one letter and the next?

Thus the book is first read outside its limits.

1

*(God is the measured and immeasurable death
of God.*

*He who has destroyed himself: what can he re-
member but notorious destructions?*

*Scream: desire of the book before the book. O
death, with you all has been said.*

*Vital knot—why do I think of vipers' knot? A
burst of sun and sea has struck the universe with
liquid fire.*
  *Does a word not die as surely of the colored poi-
son of the pen as by a pointed stone or knife? Once
finished off in its standard form, it is read, it is
born.*
  *Thus we see the beginning through Good and
Evil, the embodiment of our short-lived laws.*
  *Our birth enters the immemorial moment of the
death of God and the world.)*

He who cheated you out of your world by some trick or other deserves only violent hatred. Against the Enemy of the soul the battle
must be decisive.
  If you win you will later (no doubt because you are lonely and

tired) be indulgent with your victim, and someday, who knows, even tender. But beware of the senseless love which leads to desiring God with a passion.

He who pretends to give all deprives us of our future. Giving means opening out, means forging our tomorrows from the best in us gathered for others. God hampers universal brotherhood. He forbids man to imagine kindness.

But for those who are in love with the absolute, obsessed by eternity, turning to God to adore or destroy Him means reaching the depth of human anguish. For we are desperately driven to claim responsibility for the death of God in order to love Him more than ourselves, against ourselves.

A great love carries within it a mourning for love.

O Yaël, how I would have loved you in my misery.

2

(The word is a test, the summons a pact.

Dawn. And the end of the day. Eternity is preserved.)

3

With nothing left to invent God drowned in Himself. It would be interesting to know which was His last invention—the fatal one. Some claim it was man.

(Innocence of Evil. Could it be that original sin was, rather than a sin of knowledge, the part we played in the death of God which, for being born last, we take entirely upon ourselves?)

4

(Have I, in my hope to undo the evil that eats us,
held your head too long under water? Your child's-
head, lissom dawn and sponge?

Shore of absence where the body ran aground,
the light, free of bandied words, spreads from
mouth to ear for you, O living-dead.

You, half open at the core. In your flesh I violate
the void.)

A circle
and in the circle another
circle
and in the new circle still
another circle
and so on till
the last: a forceful
point,
then an invisible point
unbelievably present,
majestically absent.
A woman and a word.
A woman turning
around a word turning
slowly, faster,
unbelievably fast
till they are but
one circle in the space that spawned them
pursuing a smaller
and ever smaller,
grotesquely tiny circle.
A hole. An empty socket.

An eye of night.
A shattered eyeball.
And then? You look.
You plunge.
Is this what is called unity:
a circle undone?
A circular scream,
step,
and avowal?

5

*(Was it perhaps your heart, Yaël, that made me
hate God?*

I took you in as a word.

"I" is the book.)

On the 17th of March, last year, I had a dream which left me very
upset.
A woman used my life for her own ends.
"Lilith, Eve, Cressida? Which one?" Gabriel will write me later.
"The lie of God," I said to myself.
"Beautiful through death.
"No doubt ours."

6

*(One man suggests that Eve was God's first word
of love; another, on the contrary, that she was His
last.*

*Eve betrayed God
and God created night.*

*We shall seize the pathos of the lie in all its
brutality.*
O voice of rose and mud.

*Is it in the end a matter of finding out if perhaps
speech was given to us only so that we could settle
down in the lie?*
*Luckily we die of it. And against us, at the cost
of our flesh and blood, truth stamps itself in glittering negative letters*
on the blue void,
on the black nothing.

*Listen: in every vowel and every consonant
beats the pulse of the book, blankly oblivious of the
world.)*

"Wherever my voice fails the voice of the book steals in."

"Tell me, what is this voice of the book?"

"A familiar voice. Mine, maybe."

"Are you the book?"

"Am I myself?"

"Wherever the voice of the book fails yours wastes away."

"What voice could come out of the silence of the book?"

"Could you be speaking from the heart of silence?"

"Am I speech? Am I silence?"

This is a book or, rather, the hope for a book written and rewritten night after night, as if it could not come about by writing alone, as if it were happening elsewhere, far from my pen, without my patiently awaited words, with other words, other dreams, by other routes, during other rests, with other screams, but with the same silence.

This has gone on for some time. For some time I have been writing to myself because from the prelude to the end there is finally only one man. And I have gotten used to proceeding by words and in the wake of an unknown word.

So I write as one speaks to one's shadow: softly. So softly that our words sometimes merge.

As I talk to myself my words let go and plunge into silence. I am convinced that the book is a piece of land on a subsoil formed by my trapped words. Arid land. Without shade.

What can I have to say, to write, to myself? We must make a distinction: The man who talks to himself goes back over what has happened or is about to; he is angry at or (most of the time) moved by recent events or gets giddy with words never to be said by anyone else. Whereas the man who writes . . . Ah, that is a different matter.

The act of writing comes last in a series of gestures (at least three) which we tend to consider natural, but which are not always so. This puts writing at a distance from the hand in charge, which is all the greater because the ink-fed hand in turn marks, with every sentence, its distance from the person it belongs to.

You can say anything that comes into your head. You cannot (even if you try) put it that way on paper.

A man at his desk is in the position of an angler by the river. One looks for hours at an untouched sheet, the other at the water with a brighter circle on the surface, around the bait, the center of attraction. One spies on words, the other on fish. This shows what an important part the pen plays and how careful the fingers holding it must be in order not to thwart its moves and shiftings which discreetly, as if in the dark, follow the tracks of their prey and sometimes even anticipate its crossing.

I have for a long time been on good terms with words. But this does not mean that they always show a liking for me.

Some mornings I have endless trouble tackling them. Everything irritates them. We face each other like dog and cat. I am the dog, of course. My faithfulness is sorely tested lying in wait for the moment of transformation when the cat turns dog to please me.

7

Lie down, woman. You are a real woman, and I am man enough to wake you.

I can accept God only dead, just as I wanted you dead, Yaël, against a fading sky.

O how much.

The sun spares the infinite.

> (*It is said that the word can see even where no-*
> *body hears it.*
> *The sounds quietly shed light.*
> *This for your eyes, Yaël.*
> *This for our road.*)

8

You do not want to die, yet one day you will.
You do not want to lie, and yet you lie.
Man is moved from birth by frustrated desires which drive him to rebellion.
Eternity escapes him.

Stolen life is life harassed by fate, by divine fault.

A child blames his toys. Man blames man.

The hour—shadow and flame—wields its power of life and death
over the universe and man. But its minutes are numbered.

Yaël is passage and use of God, she is
the body He turned from in final retreat,
body which rots for Him of the merciless moment.
Ah, to be the moment.
To tear the skin off all words.
To speed their insides on toward the void.
To shake the flame.

A tree is a home for birds and a pain for the earth, which moves
space to pity.
This is why leaves tremble like wings and weep dew.
Strangers to one another, we only answer ourselves.

*(If fire grown cold closes the loop, does this not
admit an impossible seam at the place of death?)*

Blinding interval where dreams atone.
As far from death as from life.
We stay apart
in the face of eternity.

Where what little health a sheet of paper has leaves the words
free to die at their own hour, there we learn, Yaël, that blankness is
the simple need to lose.

(You have caught the incurable disease of the book. O my brother, let us carve our road into the void.)

9

To come outside the walls, to break free of the vise. To let my blood flower.

To compose a hymn to gardens, to birds.

O dreams and scents dear to the soul, to live by the wings and petals of the lie. Busy bees, roses already nude.

To take pleasure in my weakness and limits.

Truth is a dagger at the gate of forbidden nights.

Let me survive in what sprouts and delights in the best of the plant.

(Man of writing, you must not stop on the road. Words forbid it, and the book, O gammoning, O bowsprit, presses tight against your soul.)

Your step, Yaël. Will it ever fall in with mine?

10

(These dark spaces. You hem them with time where the infinite burrows.)

Does renunciation lead us to the truth? I tried to be true. I have not renounced anything, Yaël, not anything. On the contrary, I have wanted to own everything in order to destroy it all—but is this possible?

I have sailed with you on the suspicious sea. I have continued to write, to resort to the word which has taken your name.

My doubts, my anxieties, my cowardice, my disappointments— only your life and your voice could translate and express them.

Your reality in the book became mine. I became *the other* for you and against myself. I was your song and your echo. Will the weapon which could not touch you turn against me? I have lived the life of a dead man.

Behind the hour, behind our hour, Yaël: eternity.

Is the book the place where the hour fades into time? Then it is also the rectangle reserved for meditation in Persian gardens, where the world comes down from the four horizons to confront its fate as a celestial body with the darker fate of man.

> (*Talk of decadent literature or militant literature always makes me smile.*
>
> *The book eludes all labels. It does not belong to any clan or class. It never follows a single vein.*
>
> *It is the lonely place where the writer feels his solitude.*
>
> *Writing the book is an undertaking alien to the current ideals and the ideas we have about man and the world.*
>
> *The infinite (which is the space of the book) cannot serve as background for communication, nor eternity (which is its impass) for our exchange of opinions.*
>
> *The days of the book pass against the beat of time, pass in the margins of a sheet the size of the dream and ambition of words.*
>
> *Ah, to be color for the painter, tone for the composer, word for the writer, as, when we scan the horizon at dawn, we are without knowing it the first blaze of death.*)

All reasons for living are in the book. But the book of a life is reason's honed blade.

The word burns with its ink, Yaël, as the broken mirror of your misfortune glitters in the sun.

> (*Schism: kin to the scythe. Bread must be divided.*)

THE TIME
BEFORE THE STORY

Pulverized mirrors. The earthly paradise was asleep in the mirrors.

. . . this time before time, this strange time of God's sleep.

God was shrewd enough to forget God at every stage.

An eye. Man contends with God for an eye.

. . . and the story will be where it is expected.

My Characters In and Out of the Book

Time begins with the book.

1

(To be on your own dunghill.
To be at home in the book.

When God said: "I am who I am," must we not
understand: "I am who I was?"

Death has the folded wings of the word.

"The book is always beyond the word. It is the
place where the word dies."

"What is this word, Yaël, that has no life and
takes ours?"

"Word of the farthest sky. It makes its nest in the
book."

You write. The back of the page remains blank.

We are not free. We are nailed alive to the signs
of the book.
Could it be that our freedom lies in the word's
vain try to cut loose from the word?)

And it was the time when the star struck God dead in the star.
And it was the time when the sun struck God dead in the sun.
And it was the time when the world struck God dead in the
world.
And it was the time when man struck God dead in man.
This time is told
by Lilith and Eve
in dreams and those telling moments
when water and fire only want
to say what is
with a voice stolen from the sky,
from the lake.

> (*You go in search of the truth, and truth follows
> you. You try to cut a path in the jungle. Hostile
> vegetation. The lie protected you even while tear-
> ing your skin with its aggressive plants.*
> *Uncovered you are at the mercy of beasts.*
> *Risk of writing.*
> *Death also has virgin forests.*
>
> *Perhaps, Yaël, you had your own story to tell?*)

Yaël. Her dark hair. The frail snare of her eyes. Her secret words
mixed with insects that flee the light. Her voice revealed.
Yaël's body in the mesh of dawn. Her pearly neck, irreproachable
presence. Her shoulders, soft pebbles submerged. Her breasts circled by spring tides. Her masterful hands. Her belly of giant algae
and rose. Narrow hips. Long legs of wayward currents. Her princely
feet.
And the nights and days, voracious reality and heralding of the
eyes.
Across shadow and light goes the way to Yaël

to receive her word. For Yaël is the universal word: signs, colors, sounds of earth and sky, the chance of a grain of salt and the spiral silence of towers.

(Dreams read the ocean from the inside.

O Yaël, how can you be the joy of the world in its abundance and at the same time the scream of the waning abyss?)

I had decided to kill Yaël. I went to her room. I sat on the edge of the bed where she had just lain down. I bent over and took her head in my hands. Frightened, she stared at me the way you look at a spreading fire. My hands strangled her. God who had trembled in her was now smothered with her. I opened my fingers . . .

Everything grew dim.

To ask little of yourself means to ask little of the book. Where our reasons break down the book has the scope and rigor of an oracle. With all its illusory fullness it cannot be forced to agree.

There is an impassable space between writer and book which the readers are called on to fill. This is why the act of writing is so painful. It does not save a man, it throws him back into the void.

Only man can do something for man.

In the book, friendship is based on what is no longer, on what was once said. Friendship of one solitary word for another.

I shall always remember a bas-relief in the temple of Abydos where the god Horus and the sun-god Ra united in one body under the name Rharakhti, Horus of the Horizon, let Ramses II smell the "ankh," the symbol of life. I dreamed of my pen infusing this sign, which in ancient Egypt represented eternal life, into words so that every letter would be charged and enriched with it.

The idea grew in me that life is a gift from beyond, a present which death gives to the creature whose reign is told by image and book.

Life is the time the words need to enter the book, the time man has to exhaust words and embrace silence.

Truth of couples, the spasms of love are degrees in the void. A man who listens is most remote from the earth, a lover of mountaintops forever silent.

2

(Of all possible gestures, to keep the Gesture.

To make the blood of the night gush forth means piercing the course of the sun. Noon burns everything, but at dusk the dark displays its wounds and brings suit.

Wounds close to the vote of the ground, fields of wheat cut down. Bread tastes of the grey blood of the earth which feeds us.

Woman, your breasts out of your dress are a fever tray where, still warm, the severed head of the hero who won you bleeds.)

Yaël with blue hair. Behind glass, behind a cloud, under water. Her face recessed, blurred. But her large black eyes outside the cloud, the glass, the water. Body outlined—every page like a foggy beach, O words still grey, not yet black; every page like a blaze of morning; all shape washed out by the white of the page, her body nearly white, barely sketched in by the wrinkles on the water surface, the reflections of the glass, the imagination of the cloud.

Yaël is in the book and already in the winter of the book.

The word is a word of distance, around death.

Night answers sundown with a salvo of a myriad familiar stars.
Ah, that the song be the song of our childhood when our pains
glittered like crossed swords on the ceiling of a tiny room.

> (*I rediscover the book. So cruelly evicted, so
> steadily brought to bay by death.*)

The legless cripple lies with his missing legs. The one-armed man
lies with the arm he no longer has. The deaf-and-dumb lies with the
inarticulate sounds of his mouth. The blind man lies with his eyes in
tow of a dead look toward passes beyond waiting, beyond silence.
Breath is a lie.

Is the truth wind, violent breath? Then a conflagration would be
the truth of the flame, the ocean that of a drop of water.
O springs outdone.

What cannot be mastered would be truth by virtue of its boldness.

The legless cripple lies with the legs he invents. The one-armed
man lies with the arm his mind fits to his shoulder. The deaf-and-
dumb lies with his mouth where consonants and vowels clash. The
blind man lies with the eyes of another time, another forehead, another place.

I had decided to kill myself. I was *the other* whom I had long pursued, whom Yaël had given a face. And I let him—myself?—stran-
gle me.
Once dead, the night breathed me in . . .
Everything grew dim.

How did we come to this?

(We have no name.
Only Yaël is named.

Boundless, time is the sorrow of time.
I shall rejoin mankind at the end of time.)

The Light of the Sea

If you burn a book, it opens unto absence in the flame. If you drown it, it unfolds with the wave. If you bury it, it quenches the thirst of the desert. Because all words are pure water of salvation.

With a tree on fire the earth matches a sky full of fruit.

If we want to cross the threshold of truth we must cease to be, in the midst of what is.

Man and nature trade shadow and life.

The universe of shadows is the universe of an eye swept away in a flood. Night's consciousness: a dead star.

Absent, the creature perceives the infinite.

On the level of creation, the pupils are giant breasts.
The world is an infant to whom the eyes give suck.

At no time was the building an obstacle.
The stones are of passion,
the portal of reason.

Avoid confusing face and features. The face is omen, the features are attributes.

Tern, swallow of the sea. The ocean has its own springtime.

The book, I have to admit, is closer to an anthology than to an epic.

The light of the sea adapts to the angry as well as to the cheerful wave. It has its string of dreams and its salt tears. This central brightness which envelops the world to the point of hiding it, in the daytime, from man, is it not the space beyond the page where our frustrated thoughts move, poor worlds led astray?

If we no longer think, it does not mean we stop thinking. Thought is the conscious and unconscious of the world. When a musician stops playing on his instrument it does not mean he no longer hears the sounds of the work he played. The brain takes the place of the ear. Memory revives with each note that is found again.

Have I lived in my memory? Is this how I remember so precisely a slice of vagabond life which I can hardly believe I lived? *The other*'s life, yet mine in Yaël's wake whose face changed so constantly that every instant claimed it as its own. Thus our memories give us back our words, and we question the signs they gather for us to meditate on. Facing an accomplished fact we push our self-questioning through writing to the dimmest borders of the being that escapes us. We die a death for two where the book is born.

In the book, order is primeval whereas disorder is the systematic refusal to complete the work which every page reinforces with its void.

Making a book or, rather, helping it to come into being means above all blurring its utopian tracks, wiping out footprints. Then the word takes the place still warm from the heel. And we go to the word and with it retrace our silent, forgotten way, a way taken for and without it.

The book commands, and we guide the book. A writer's life is a steady march toward a star. The constellations answer for his work. Black stars, which recall night, lined up for what festivities? On the page they no longer shine for the eye but for the mind.

"My eyes will be my thoughts, and my hands my road," said the stranger whose voice sounds like mine when I create.

Improvised paths of the eyes: a shadow mourns for a thing. Once its preeminence is expressed, appearance rejects appearance.

In the name of His creatures God accepts the world of a foreboding glimmer which like a gold dot blinking in space reveals in flashes (O moving solitude) the imperceptible broken line of death.

Fear of Time

This anxiety to write which clings to the time of writing.

1

(Being born means looking for your name; find-ing it means you are dying.

God died of believing in His eyes.

A man's life is the passage from death's shadow to death.

Man speaks and sees in the other.

O time of instinct.
Distinct instant.
O time of the other.)

Once formulated, the word breaks open, and we see that it con-tained a silence of the end of time into which it hurls us. Whereas we had hoped to get to the end of words as well as to the end of ourselves and the world. We had hoped, our souls heavy with want-ing to be born and love, heavy with waves thirsting for sky, to say the salt and the undone dream.

Entering into yourself means finding a void. Entering into a word means finding absence. Opalescent doors. We must only consider the passage from sky to sky.

Does man find man in silence? Little by little the way gives up the way, and the world finds itself where it is not.

Man's fate is heavy because our actions are gratuitous from the start, passing shadows on a surface bathed in light. But the day has its hours and its rhythm. All encounters are gratuitous, and so are, in the lives we consider, the events which break or carry them.

Dawn is more than a hope, it is an elect full of fresh fervor. Straining towards what is to come, his ties cut, man when he is finally free gorges himself on eternity. His gravity lies in being available and great, in the vacancy of a moment which will fuse with his life. Not to expect anything and yet to die daily of infinite expectation.

A serious man is not necessarily a grave man. Some kinds of gravity flower at the heart of euphoria.

In his will to know man condemns innocence and with it all reference to gravity. But the essential part of knowing cuts us off from the tree of knowledge and opens unlimited possibilities for chance.

Man's chance is his ability to wonder. He gets it from death which annuls and reveals.

Surprise (letting yourself be surprised, becoming passive, reaching by and by a total receptivity) is the sap of creation and its pact. You cannot build on what you have already seen, already thought. But you see and think as you dig, as you build, as you complete. For completion is another beginning.

Death is the gratuitous act *par excellence*. Creating means imitating death which is God's daring and imagination. Death is in everything which will be tomorrow, so that man's quest of the absolute has to go through it.

The letters of the alphabet are contemporaries of death. They are stages of death turned into signs. Death of eternal death. But there are other signs which the letters covet, erased signs reproduced by gestures at the heart of what is named. Thus the bird's take-off contains all forms of flight. And is it not also the bird which, as it cuts through the sky, writes and repeats the universal "delete" which rules our fate? Ah, the written world dies and is reborn of the bird.

Gravity is therefore a consciousness, outside time, of the time of death which is neither a ruined time nor detours of an undated challenge, but a return to the world of margins and miracles from which man is forever ejected as from a loving womb after he has been molded, a weak foetus, in its dark flesh.

The birth of a star is like that of a child. Space contracts and projects innumerable universes closed within their dazzled death. Do I claim one human being corresponds to a whole starry sky? Eternity is based on an initial explosion of the universe. To a starry sky correspond generations of men, reproducing forever. Perhaps the last man will die with the last star.

Becoming conscious of death means denying any hierarchy of values which does not account for the stages of darkness where man is initiated into the mysteries of night. Death is both the loss and the promise of a hope which day wears itself out courting at every moment. To be or not to be in the absurd agony of a secret glimmer until morning.

All agony is the painful gestation of a world fashioned by the fever and limits of the soul, unveiled by gasps and sighs.

What will our future be made of? Life does not consider itself useless and vain. Through it, death will go to its death.

Creatures in their will to live reconcile their days with the death of the sky. Thus man and the universe have the same future. But neither sky nor man can know for sure the moment (or the thousand moments) of their end, the fatal second when they will forever cease to die. They will be destroyed in the moment they least expect it. Hence becoming conscious of death does not mean going straight towards it, but, on the contrary, plunging into life to take on its ochre renewals.

For the universe is first of all a spectrum of colors. They fade, one after another, as a shout weakens in its echos and joins the world's immense reservoir of silence where the stars riveted to their rays come to slake their thirst.

2

> (*To live, to write allows death to move like the
> pen in a hand, like the sap in a stem.*
>
> *. . . then I thought of a work which would con-
> tinue into the night, where all would be dead be-
> fore being born, where the story would be like a
> fruit of the tree of death.*)

To kill God in a supreme combat is one of the impossible tempta-
tions man falls into.

God is *before* and *after* God. God died in creating, in creating
Himself, that is to say in multiplying His death.

Creation consecrates God and man and, hence, their void. To be
a sea for the unfurling octopus. To be a sky for the miracle of stars.
The void is an element favorable to both existence and death.

If I killed, which half of myself would win out over the other?

I die for all words, in every vocable.

Absurd gesture which has already taken place in vain, yet neces-
sary gesture for him who set out to die of his own end.

In the book, the words fall like birds struck by lightning for having thought they could wrest a piece of sky from the infinite.

Eternity has stolen their breath and made them hard the better
to swallow them.

Thus our body, while it lasts, helps us to founder more quickly.

I now believe (and I have come to see this as a truth on which the
book's reality depends), I now believe that narrative in the usual
sense is not the business of the book, that it is extraneous to the
book.

The writer who declares himself a novelist or storyteller does not
serve the book; he does not care about it for one moment and even
considers it less than nothing.

A novel is the writer's triumph over the book, and not the opposite, because the novelist makes a strong entrance with his char-

acters and, with them as go-betweens, gives free rein to his innumerable voices. The book is trampled by them, its voice choked by theirs.

The desert, scorning distance, reveals any presence of man or beast to the ear of the nomad who sleeps on the sand. Thus the book brings the world into view through our hearing. Step by step, and as if coming out of silence.

You cannot go towards the truth, which admits the void, by winning wars. You can only go there by losing them. This is why every great book leaves us empty-handed. Miserable and empty-handed.

The day I shall write a novel I shall have left the book, have lost it. But I shall not be without shame. I shall not boast of my victories, shall not display my muscles in public. I shall ask my voice to stay humble so that, even while cutting itself off from its branches it might, one day, down at the roots, find again the voice of the bruised earth and the page.

Shared death, search of harmony. Writing a book means joining your voice with the virtual voice of the margins. It means listening to the letters swimming in the ink like twenty-six blind fish before they are born for our eyes, that is to say, before they die fixed in their last cry of love. Then I shall have said what I had to say and what every page already knew. This is why the aphorism is the deepest expression of the book: it lets the margins breathe, it bears inside it the breath of the book and expresses the universe at the same time.

This agreement with words, this previous agreement with the book remain my worry and care.

Here in the shady paths of a beginning work which already rejects me, how could I not pay for the failure of a book impossible to write and yet written at the heart of words which soon, at their end and mine, I shall not be able to break or follow.

Man rising up against God is neither victim nor hangman. He is grappling with death in a region where living and dying are synonyms.

The word of the book comes from the white borders which the universe sustains with its mastery of the deep.

A wise man (an adept of Hassidism disowned by the members

of his community) taught me to doubt words because—this is my interpretation—syllables are enslaved and only a part of the truth which vainly tries to be true. Elsewhere, this wise man praised as a virtue the song of hope that rises out of the silence of words. But how come these joyful songs have such a strain of sadness they sound like sobs? It is because they are songs of dead words, eternal words which we humans cannot hear.

The bottom of silence is a bit of cold air which no wind ever moves. But the void makes the world turn.

Yaël, *the other* and myself, one and the same end . . .

Remains to be seen if it really is possible to make the book.

Letter to Gabriel (fragments)

3

They had chosen my head for their gathering. You could see mostly their teeth, eburnean bars behind which words seemed forever prisoner. They said more or less the following:

"You too want to kill God.
You too have dreamed of killing God.
You too thought you had killed God.
You too.
Just like us.
And you will soon cry victory
as we did.
And you will soon think you are free
as we thought we were.
You will mow down the wheat of light.
You will tear down the huge tents of night.
You will break the storm lanterns
and make a phantom people
elect you Prince of the world.
You will rule a desert world,
O fool like us.
You will have lost

friend and beloved,
providential gesture
and crystalline word
which you named with one name in two:
Ya-El,
a call more harrowing than a scream,
a call from God to God
to perish of coupling syllables,
to die of your hands
and your ludicrous plan."

Then one who had been dead for more than a thousand years came forward and said:

"All roads start out from you and return to their point of departure.
"You are the probable day, the open night whence we come, where we go."

Then one who had been dead for a thousand years came forward and said:

"The desert. If you should, one day, discover a blade of grass there it is because the sand was betrayed by water or by man.
"You have sacrificed trees, do you understand?
"May the sand be your salvation."

Then one who had been dead for more than a century came forward and said:

"White peace of the well.
"Water tames the doves.
"Ah, consider that the most famous monogram is, elsewhere, only a tiny fern."

Then one who had been dead for a century came forward and said:

"Endured suffering, shed tears, joys of a moment. When I wanted to express you I was only listening to another man's song of pain and joy."

Then one who had been dead for a year came forward and said:

"My life was written with white words from the tip of a lance."

But he was answered: "That is absurd. Does white not mean absence?"

Then one who had just died came forward and said:

"A lie is the time of the dream of God's death.
"Your death in *the other* was my death."

> (*The laugh of the dead. Most cruel to take.*
> *It rises from the ground, and our tears water it,*
> *O hideous plant of hellish seasons.*)

"Put out the lights," I screamed, "put them out, suns, lights under glass. Blow out all flames.
"Death bends over death
"and kisses its lips."

4

> (*You do not know where death will lead you. You are alive.*
>
> "*Night is old, more so than day, by twelve times the veiled hour.*"
> "*By twelve tarnished centuries, by twelve times the centuries.*"

"*Ah, time means separation, and we live in time.*"

First I thought of death as a forlorn orphan girl, then as a beloved woman. Later both child and woman slowly withdrew with the landscape, with the world, and I could not catch up. I was nailed to one of the hypothetical peaks of a dream, in the void, although I had not stopped running. This is no doubt how it is with the flame of a candle blown out, with a tarnished star listening for its light lost in the distress of an engulfed world. So now death seems to me the immensely lonely shadow of what was.

The joys and misgivings of the sea are those of the water, but hundredfold.
One day the sea learned that its color came from the void. Ah, how it leapt up to touch the sky. Thus man, odorless, colorless man, throws himself into the void to soak up the smell of time, to take on eternity's color.

God is female in His words, male in His gestures.

Has man invented God in order to give a higher sense to his beliefs? But God lies and thus resembles His creature.
And it was spread all over the world that God had formed man in His image.)

To repeat in front of the white page: "You will see what I shall put there." For whom? Nobody is listening.

A book is an education. Where will this one lead me? I owe it an approach to the lie through the anxieties of a couple meandering toward death.

Wellspring and seed are the vices of truth.

The world rises up on the horizon in its bold light or its nightly nothing.

Shapes disappear into their shadows, that is, into their future.

Fidelity is future's fury.

> (*The ways of the eyes are the ways of our burdens.*
>
> *All the distance of stars is in writing by night. In the morning, the word becomes the link of a new chance.*
>
> *You know yourself, man with death for your head.*)

This work (which could have had a more complete title: *Yaël or the Death of God*) has two parts: *The Time before the Story* which is its portion of dark, its prophetic part, and *The Time of the Story* which is the journal of the death of a being in the ambiguous *other*, that is, in the alternating of All and Nothing which appearance tries to mask.

Denouncing appearance, the bait where God waits to die, means going to the truth of the void, straight into the heart of absence.

For God died of looking. The eyes record the lie of images. Mirror of a mirror, the universe lives by reflections. Trees proudly on their guard are the blossoming time of shadows, and the glass reflects the dreams of gardens.

Yaël embodies the principle of life. In her, the world dies with man wherever the book is written.

> (*Once the word belongs only to the book we shall be dead.*

. . . but how come we forget the words of the book?

Could they be living words?

In that case you have not carved anything, and your words are shadows thrown by words.

Words of eternity. With life driven out. Take life with you, man. A book is a stela nobody can place.

Will I one day speak in your silence, Yaël?)

The Long Dialogue of Centuries

"All limits depend on light. Is God not the first,
the original dark, in that case?
"And the first light to fathom the dark?"

"God is the all-embracing center."

The other is the savage sense of the sun.

"The light shows many a kindness to the lie, yet truth is in the
light."

"The dark is dead passion, destroyed desire. Night loves the night
with its radiance in mourning."

"Silence is truth. Refusing to give, it gives us to see.
"God is silence."

"God does not see. He is entrenched behind what is seen."

"God cannot be held back. He is the extreme of inconceivable
sight."

"And extreme darkness which gives us to ourselves in absence."

"The invisible is both renunciation of the lie and the will to one
only truth."

"Mute melody of worn memories. Rust is fire on vacation. From the beginning, the hour has trusted the sea."

"The hour in its darkness is a binary measure. We live in two times. Presence and absence take turns as its face."

"And neither face ever rules the other. So that the truth of the hour is a dizzying lack of being."

". . . an oblique opening."

"So that man in his flesh and his thoughts exists where eternity leaves him behind."

". . . where God is man's Truth which He withdraws."

". . . because death is life's first blood."

". . . because death is the second life of God."

"Thus the instant became the breath of the creature who burns and consumes himself in his breath."

"Life continues beyond the day. Chased out of the garden in order to regain it (it will not be the same garden; it will only look the same) the instant, in every pulse beat of the world, is a rhythmic word.

"Thus the tree is aglow with a thousand similar words."

"Truth often is rhythm. Man and universe participate in one joint existence."

"The hour repudiates the hour, and eternity grows."

"Margins are the lips of the well of time where death draws water."

"Thus a river pushes at the weakest point of the bank. And the grass grows and bends with the same water, with long patience."

"Thus flows time outside time."

"Do we pay for the sin of knowledge by having our eyes torn out? Appearance condemns us to appearance."

"Impossible truth. Invincible truth. The possible carries truth, but outside its limits."

"Going towards truth means going all the way. It means crossing all borders in order to look at them from the other side. Truth remains what is reached."

"Worthy conquest of man where God takes refuge, rejected from His Creation."

"God is not in the hand held out to another hand."

"Grasping means accepting things as they appear, imposing and exchanging them in their conventional form, appreciating the latter as the only one or pretending to . . ."

"Reality is not in our hands. Touching a thing, our fingers and palms play at creating the illusion of a reality which can be caught in its still movement."

"How ingenious desire is in its forms and caresses."

"Lies obey our touch. The senses have disqualified God and His essential insensibility, but have consecrated man without God."

"The body remains a crossroad."

"'Cut off the hands,' howls the fool year after year. 'So the eyes can kindle.'"

"What is not grasped has all the chances to become real."

"We chat, waiting for time. Alas, we are only marking time."

"Thus the word hardened as it lasted."

"Thus the stone became flint.
"Anything expressed is above all a rose of sound. And the world will never fit in a word."

"And God never stays One and the same as you approach."

"Each for himself and both fused in the crystal of an idyllic mirror. Seen, but not delivered."

"Identity is distant. What is contemplated begins to contemplate."

"Any fruit is an artificial star. You taste the manure of the abyss. And soon the birds take off in fright."

"Where are we when we fall silent? The word is the presence of a forgotten presence."

". . . and the first gulp from the well and the course of the divide."

"But what is promised soon grows dim here, as if the infinite were a crowning feast."

"But here the mirrors band together to reflect forever man's last cry, his final cry for help. Here, the world in falling destroys the world."

"Here man brings suit against the word on which he has thrown himself for the most beautiful love song."

"Here man, with his soul in despair, leaves the word and shivers."

"Distance is the truth of speech."

"The wall with its coat of plaster is eaten by the sky. Thus glaciers rise in the whiteness of death.
"O harsh bed of snow, calm rind amazed by transparency."

"Sheltered from the day, man faces his shadow."

"We shall celebrate gardens. Spread mirrors. Glorify God."

"God is at the back of the mirror and at the heart of the tree."

"And the word, beseeched and denied, will be the axe man lifts against God."

"And man will perish by the axe."

"O time of the Witness, red spider silence."

The Three-paneled Mirror

God wears the mask of nobility.

There are no wounds caused by truth. Only the lie can touch us.

What strikes us is our truth, but truth rejects that.

So man turns to God and blasphemes. And the blasphemy falls back on him.

For God is the dawn of an exhausted wing.

A mask on a wall: maybe our face for eternity.

You will die in a mirror.

1

"He is the One who sees things as they are," man was told when he despaired of seeing.

In the first mirror, she smiles. She thinks of the treasure in her womb, of the life she is handing on and whose image moves her.

She has been in this village for six months. Waiting. Nobody has come to see her.

She looks out of the window at the hilly landscape where the trees are still asleep on their feet. The sun is barely coming up.

In the second mirror, her scream has cracked the glass—or was it

the object she thought she had thrown at the door so that her landlady should hear?

People are fussing around her. A doctor and two peasant women.

"She has to be taken to the hospital. It's urgent," orders the doctor. Twenty or thirty miles away.

In the third mirror, the void engulfs the room.

Thighs spread wide.
The lips of the void, a vagina, huge.
Moist at the call of the phallus, bleeding as it rejects the world.
Life gambled and lost.
A dead infant, a box with a broken lock.
What was in this scorned casket?
Roads and roads and roads.

A thousand beings die with every newborn.
There is rotten fruit among the seeds.

2

A blatant milestone on the road to death.
The first.
You will go from face to face, but your breast will never feed the
child of your love.
Maimed mother.

The child you wanted to rock remains the most loved.
The creature atones.

In the first mirror, O woman, the lie relished its spite.
In the second mirror, O woman, the lie blew up.
In the third mirror, O woman, truth questions itself.

3

She has eyes of stone in the falling rain.
I do not yet exist.

Stretched out across the dark
she records, forms a sphere.

What if space were only an immense yawning dawn?
God is bored.

4

In the first mirror, childhood found the garden laid waste.
In the second mirror, innocence found the roots in flame.
In the third mirror, it is dark, so dark that you tremble.

You will go from image to image, for God's amusement.

5

An insect tests the circle of light, a bird the basic line.

The dark speaks to the dark:

"Choosing means fixing? Then the lie is the night of choice."

"If reality means choice only the day is real."

"You grasp. You finger. You grope.
"You bring on day."

"Black oil, night of how many stories? Stain, stream, sura?"

The dawn speaks to the dawn:

"Does every thought rest on a vegetable wager?"

"Time has the body for witness."

"Sea anemone, garden made of flowering water."

"You will die. Time will not see itself again."

Man speaks to man:

"Always the book and me. Unavoidable confrontation."

"The soul is a breath of death, a head airy with eternity."

You will go from word to word into the silence of God.

6

She noted:

"I looked out of my window at the mountains where the trees were studding the sky with stars."

She noted:

"Tree, I can see you.
You lie to my eyes.
I know you by the slant of your looks.
Not your existence: your impertinence."
"Who is more impertinent than a liar?"
"You lie to my mind.
Yet truth is *before* or *after* pact and seeing,

or perhaps *between*.
Tree, I watch you.
Struck by your smallest trait. ·
Every day I feel closer to you
in what you are not and what your name designates.
Tree, I am growing with you,
with wanting to love
your bark and leaves."

7

The garden has folded its wings on us. Warm dark of the nest.
The branch broke. Morning caught us helpless.

You will go from penny to penny until the end of time.

"And you will be blind. And you will rock the boat. And you will
hate each other because of her, and you will love each other to the
bitter end. I shall be pleased not to see and to die of myself in your
retinas."
Thus speaks the Voice in the time of absence.

The Garden

Seeing now means seeing only Nothing.

God's knowledge is in the tree.

Hence Nothing rules All. God is Nothing. Nothing is a ring.

I shall lead you into death and we shall forget the age of gardens.

1

Wisdom of symbols. A book which makes us see is a book of great wisdom.

You will make my body your favorite garden.

Every grain in its rich hours has to make the grade of a spiked lure.

Thinking about the terrestrial paradise leads us to a reflection on gardens.

Before they had a landscape, man and woman had a park cultivated by the Lord.

THE BOOK OF QUESTIONS

Trees would have come into being before the animals if the latter had not been sure of a body even while still absent.

With exemplary subtle touch, every inch of seeded ground perpetuates a human moment through the asides of form which are its symbolic paths. As if the body were eternity.

Henceforth the couple will subdue the world with their intuitive return to the beginnings. They will see and carry on for the universe.

The lie is at its ease among plants. With its help, leaves and flowers resemble one another. The lie reproduces the same face.

Man is a reflection of the garden.

2

Truth is a leaven to God's hate. For a truthful being is His equal.

Paradise lost is followed by deserts where truth, the virtue of the sand, refutes the attributes of God.

Death opens the book with which man counters death.
God is against God.

3

We must give death time to learn how to die.

4

The daydreams of people walking in a garden wrap it in a silken melancholy which is ruffled by the cold as much as by the sun.

On cloudy days, hunched under their umbrellas, people look only at the ground.

Flowers, bright, colored cups. In spring and summer they owe their perfume to their liquor. In fall, in winter, water and snow break them and hoot.

A child does not listen to trees. He makes them listen, draws them into his games.

Innocence of ambush. Revolt and resignation wear the same gala uniform. Parade without surprise.

The rainbow frays in deaf, dim reminiscences.

Painting is a shared promise. A body is a nimble palette on legs (interchangeable brushes) to walk around the world. Until night is unsealed by sleep. O dream of dreams.

The daydreams of people walking in a garden turn into brown spittle on the branches, into dew on the leaves.

The blue of the sky is the blue of the space inside roots. It turns green in trunk and stem. The fruit swells with the infinite.

Up there, the dark makes sure of the harvest. Wheat is feverish like a flame. Gathered. Winnowed. The grain sparkles.

How winsome the stars. They already smell the bread of dawn.

5

Parks have their fountains where thirst gives way.

Children have their favorite gardens. Likewise the walkers who come to inquire after the progress of vertigo in the soul of plants.

Is it the secrets the plants tell us which deliver them into our hands? Then everything would be words, and landscape these forms caught by the ear.

6

A gathering of young girls is the body of my beloved.
My mouth and fingers cull their words.

This morning, bench after bench full of girls.
A garden is the body's true world.

Girls whispering, singing, laughing.
The sad girl, is she a tear?

The more mysterious: the more voluptuous.
How small they are all to have room in one.

Yet it is the body wins out over life.
Not thought, nor pressing acts, nor work.

Radiant body, the blind man's kingdom.
What is the body? Do we ever ask?
It gives in to the eye from outside, to the hand in cahoots, gives in like the world.
Well-kept secret: the world was never more than a mooring buoy in the night.

7

Saved by the unknown, man plunges into the unforeseeable. He has no recourse but ignorance with its boastful beacon. To see by the pinhole beam.

Beautiful summer of death.
O sun of endings.

8

That face of undefinable hunger which we must resemble, is that the soul?
Tragic duplicity of our features.
God flees.

Our eager hands try in vain to hold Him back and, coming together, outline the oval of His vanished face.

9

A lie: truth making a false start?
An unhappy truth, then.
Or a good start but which, in the heat of action, in full career,
loses interest in the goal or, rather, gradually substitutes other goals
until it is formally replaced.
But for whom?
Lie: trump of profit, space where truth explodes into myriads of
countertruths which man lights up with a short-lived life.
The creature is overwhelmed.

At the end of dreams truth kills itself. The lie triumphs.
Heyday of suicide.
You cannot count on anything.
You only survive ashes.

10

A thousand earthen octopuses devour the universe.
The tree's wound is the same as the ocean's.

Was my truth the anchor of my life?
I find myself where I fell asleep.
Yaël, waking bears your name. And your body is a long shiver of
amorous flights.

11

The walker dissolves into his journeys. Years are towlines carried off by the current. The ground is suddenly no longer solid where the rose bends to look at itself. So little water. So much. Thirst performs the miracle of giving the world the privilege of dreams.

To drink. To drink the air, the dark, the day.

12

A life without miracles is doomed to the dullness of stagnant water. It has the dragonfly's capers to wake it.

On a different, but equally reduced plane, dust knows from birth the feel of downtrodden old age.

Rejected, it only irks our itinerary. Exile is its rest.

13

A garden stripped by the sun gives little jumps of modesty full of fragrance.

The leaf disclaims the branch, and the flower the stem's invitation to exhibit herself. Pranks of the birds, a piece of invisible clothing in their beaks.

The star you discover is perhaps a pale cry of love.

14

In the garden, I do not have my tree. I have neither familiar bench nor flower,
no man or woman for company.
I have nothing.
Complex net of rest.
We do not get off the earth.

I wait for oblivion within me,
oblivion with clipped wings.

15

The man walking in the garden passed Yaël: God revealing Himself as a woman or Satan with the clear eyes of God.

The trees had brought her. The grass sighed under her feet.

Shadow of a twig? Shadows are dark daggers. This is why the
murderer throws away his weapon once the crime is done.

Everywhere.

But what murder are we talking about?

Will I get the better of the unscrupulous mouth, pirate pupils,
mutinous breasts and hands?

Truth is the order of the dying.

The Death of God

The tree of knowledge bore wormy fruit. Did God know this?

Adam ate the apple with its acid taste of defiance.

Henceforth he would live and die by fighting against God, by relentlessly struggling with himself.

"You loathe Him who created the mortal world for you and who, to help you live, hides you from yourself.

"The universe belongs to him who survives it.

"In that respect, the lie is our greatest blessing.

"You reject what consoles you. O fool, you will suffer more than God if He exists. For truth is the mirage of a summit which our mountains point toward."

"I shall kill God for his cowardly goodness."

Vertigo of truth. Fatal call of the void.

Divine compassion. Dazzling blindness.

One day, ignorance was admitted into the love of the world

1

"To kill God. The master of mirrors. The father of gardens."

"Pushed by I do not know what mad, unsuspected force. With my hands.
"For my salvation and the world's. To kill God."

"Through you the world will be avenged."

"There comes a moment when the creature of severance can no longer resist his desire to cut off, at the end, the false words which have intoxicated his life. They are a peg-ladder to hell.

2

"Ungrained night. Night of murder.
"I shall not extend the deadline."

"To kill God in His original light, the stars."

"To kill God in His brazen strength, the sun."

"To kill God in His major reflection, the moon."

"The pedigreed birds are eaten by envy."

3

"To kill God in the mouth of the man struck down, in the belly of the unfaithful woman."

"You will tear God to pieces in the trusting eyes of the child."

"In stones and apples, in polluted streams, in the wind. I rage.
"I have acquired this right and take responsibility."

"Where will the world go without God? Where will the word go
without echo, buffeted by the waves?"

"The boarding was no routine visit this time. Emptied of cargo
and crew, the ship was sunk. Dynamited."

4

"God exploded? Who will announce it? Not the smallest scratch
on the skin of air or water to indicate He was struck. Nor the slightest
damage to clouds or sand. No trace of revealing smoke. Nothing
among the waves but the screams of men fighting with death."

"Shaken for a moment by the explosion, sky and sea now again
vouch for a destiny without God and stranger to the individual."

"Divinity is a duty of man's, sharpened by dialogue."

"Becoming conscious of the unity of the universe: does this not
mean retracing God's involucrate existence, inventing a center for
the void?"

5

"I have tracked all the points of assembly."

"Who is still speaking around us?
"Who is still writing over there?"

"Lie of God's, I am on your trail."

"Who could imply a name of refuge or birth? Who would dare even to sketch it?"

> *(Because I could no longer say your name, Yaël, I decided to kill.*
>
> *Then all that has a name tried to discard it, hoping to escape its awful fate. Fearful or rebellious preys, they did not know that their innocence furnished me with a sword which would run them through and through.*
>
> *The fearful die of fear, and the rebels of their revolt.*

> *Silence.*
>
> *Truth called for a mirror. For one whose three panels would be untroubled by thought. So I killed it.*
>
> *One life will do to hurl life down the abyss. One bell without clapper, to lay out the dark. The knell will do. And the serious injury.)*

6

"Let the roof fall, and chimney and lightning rod with it.
"Let the day bury the day."

"Fire runs the feast which it reduces to ashes."

"Fire. God of flames. The late God consumed in Himself, in fire. I spit my love out with the wood, I pour my hate with the melting ore."

"This age is without language."

"Silence.
"Steps get used to steps, and hands to handles."

"Silence.
"Words test God. Man is written in silence."

>(*Is God, whom man allowed to enter eternity in
his place, the beginning and end of an irreverent
meditation on the human condition which would
tend to prove that any place where people die is a
latent source of anguish?*
>
>*The hope to be saved by writing would then be
born of the word received as revelation of a non-
place, born of the book as of a space summing up
incommensurate reason.*
>
>*You play a dangerous game, Yaël: game which
the word plays forever with Passion and Thought
for partners and whose outcome is always fatal for
one of the players.*
>
>*Life is a porous word, and death probably with-
out writings.*
>*Then each page of the book is coated with un-
deniable night.*
>*But who will decipher the message of the dark
with constellations for characters?*
>*Language beyond language.*
>*Book after all books.*)

THE STORY

In the morning of flesh, death joins the death of the world.

Thus the sap assents to the sapwood.

God is the death of man, and man a moment in the graven death of God.

Ringing song of men. Campanula, the bluebell, will be my flower.

God
or the thunder that was His voice,
or the lightning that was His gesture,
or the delicate cloud He once was,
or the sky, air, water that together are His
    absence,
or fire which is pain.
our pain, Yaël,
our real and great pain.

O death, your eyes will be mine, and my freedom that of the prow.

Rice fields of the night. At dawn, tireless women with naked arms and thighs fill their baskets with stars.

Factual truth means only that others (and we ourselves) accept our interpretation of an event.

The samphire is the queen of rocks. Passion dislodges stones.

Yaël's Death

O Yaël, proscribed word.

Her first name intrigued me from the moment I heard it.

Sun of Nuriel and Uriel, master of Tahariel, Padaël, Raziel. It also reminded me of Jofiel, Zagzaguel, Achatriel, Raphaël. But it was a woman who bore it, and I realized I would love Yaël in the lips of the black crater of her name.

Countenance of God, O infinite effacing of the Face.

I remember she had her hair down that morning so that it covered her back. Black hair with a soft blue shimmer. My hand passed through it, now like a sturgeon, now like a starfish.

She was lying down. I had lifted her head with one hand, and this hand was life and its five roads, and her head was the globe.

The middle road is the hardest to follow. The longest in time. Road of noon or midnight, both day and night have set and colored it.

Was I going to explore the world by taking all its roads? But were these roads? At most, signs that people had passed this way. And even at that I was not sure they could be trusted.

Her nightgown (as if dawn were always wandering over her body) kept me from touching her. I stroked her breasts, but they were veiled breasts; I stroked her belly, but it was a veiled belly. Except for her face, only her neck and shoulders were of flesh. And her arms.

She did not react. Was she already dead or half-dead, engulfed? Heavy in the water, covered with algae, between two waves near the shore?

I was determined to save her. There was not a minute to lose. I would lay her down on the sand and make her breathe again.

I remember that morning, at dawn—or was it another morning just as grey, elsewhere, in another room?

> (. . . *in the void perhaps, land of strange souls, or elsewhere, as in a dream, in a land so far from mine that I do not know its name, and yet so attractive. Voluptuous female body the size of a continent, land like a nape or a breast with borders of down, pale land between two rings like those under the eyes of lovers which betray an infinite longing for the dark . . . ?*)

That morning—we often stayed up late after dinner, at home, or with friends in some bar—that morning or that night, I do not remember which, when she had drawn the curtains, undressed, and put out the chandelier for the dimmer bedside lamp, I lay down beside her in bed. She did not budge, braced in her refusal.

There was a gentle plush or felt animal in a corner. You could not say for sure if it moved or lay still, but you could clearly hear it breathing. It seemed a wounded beast whose breath was closer to a rattle and near whom you could have found traces of blood.

Frozen in the rim, in the edge of light outlined in the mirror, cheek against cheek, temple against temple, we could have been taken for the image of what rare coin or ivory medallion in its padded frame ready to be nailed to the wall: the effigy of the Monarch and Queen, of the conqueror and his favorite.

Was it me or *the other* embracing her? *The other*, no doubt, whom Yaël always spoke to, always looked at with so much kindness that it hurt me deeply. However, that morning or that night, I do not remember which, something strange happened which I cannot get out of my mind. I was no longer the same. I was no longer myself. I was *the other* or, rather, I finally took his place and was so excited, so grateful to the auspicious hour and the whole world that I lost control and pressed Yaël to myself so long that she collapsed without a sign of life.

I plunged into her eyes now without limits. I prayed for the moment when her lids would close and I would stop rolling through the void. I felt light, but condemned beyond remedy. I would kill myself soon, at the end of the night, and it would be the brutal end of a being who had never known why he lived.

Yet, without being absolutely sure, I think I remember being not only worried about myself. I was anxious about Yaël's death more than about my own.

My soul was stricken with remorse, bruised.

How did I manage to seize Yaël's wrist? I found myself in the bedroom, my arm against the sheet. I convinced myself that her pulse was still beating. Her life gave me back my life just as her death had hurled me toward my own.

I remember I closely examined my hands before questioning them as the Officer would do once he arrived with his "What do you have to say for yourself?"—but of course I did not do it as efficiently because I do not know the police methods of investigation.

I would say—but would I defend myself? I did not feel the need—I would say: "Yaël . . ." as if I were still speaking to her, but for the last time. I would say: "I would have liked to help you, Yaël, because that way I would have acted in keeping with my soul. I do not know if I killed you or if you died on the threshold of an impossible love, on the margins of my death." The Officer would refuse to let me get off this easily, and he would be right. But do I know what happened that night or that morning? I do not remember.

There was Yaël in bed and I beside her. I had taken her face in my hands, and her eyes were so hard, so cruelly, so stubbornly hard that the few words I heard seemed to be pronounced by her pupils.

I put out the lamp. It was light in the room. Had I pushed open the shutters to let a ray of moon in? The dark lifted at the borders of a whiter dark. But perhaps it was really morning and we were still asleep, morning welcomed through the lids of a lazy awakening, lids so thin, so nearly transparent that we kept them half-closed in order to savor the soft fore-light, the freshness of a rosy dark.

Propped on my elbow, I looked at Yaël. My face above hers was the corner stone of a crumbling wall, the eye of a storm like the center of a celestial wound which plunged the world into terror. She screamed. Getting away from me, keeping me at a distance with all the strength of her stretched arms, was her way of escaping destruction and death. Under the weight of my chest her arms gave, little by little. Then there was nothing to keep us apart but the moisture of our bodies in their untidy nakedness.

I was no longer *the other*. He stood behind me. I realized that the immense distance Yaël had tried to put between us canceled the apparent distance between *the other* and me, so that I was the nightmare she fought by clutching her lover across my hands which did not let go of her neck. Her eyes told him her love, told him her repulsion for me. They told him her faithfulness beyond death.

I turned. I was alone. With silence for an accomplice. Yaël's screams hung on the ceiling like game hung up by their legs. The sky had been pulled down with those poor beasts.

Journal I

Brief ceremony, perfidious pact: dark and light, rivals up to now, are conspiring to give the lie to the auguries.

You have more than one face.
You have taken your time.
The best part of the minute is absence.

The time of silence absorbs our time.

The body bears grudges against absence which make me think of how sullenly the moment faces eternity.

If death is in the sea its bottom is gold.
O waves swelling with life, tides with a skin of sun.
Morning is everywhere.

Those whom you see ruling are not always the rulers.

The locks of life have the dark for key.
All passage is under the sign of loss.

All waiting waits on death.
Night does wonders.

Night in every knot.
Against props.
The port a pit.

Universality of the face. The features are forgotten notches and highlights.

To honor the oracle. You construct. You trust
what is opaque and solid.
The stone reaches the clouds through stone.

The sky is coming down. Ants bustle over the
firmament.

1

My night was twined into the thread of a hellish dream.
I was at the same time Yaël, myself and *the other*.
I spoke in three voices.
I marched along three roads.
Three hearts gave orders in my chest.
But I had my eyes,
my legs and my hands,
and I was alone.

Cursed, I was both villain and vilification.

The man of the letter is threefold. In the book, there were the
man and the woman. Both struggled in the night of *the other*.
The history of the book was and will be. Likewise our history.

The soul carries alone the wing load of spreading words and the sleeping secret of dreams.

Very restless all day. I am less and less certain I dreamed it all. As if I had not been marked by a dream yesterday, but by the seal of a mysterious reality which till now I had kept secret.

Eternity is getting smaller. It lives by the real fraction of the second, and the second by its relation to the body.

In the mystery of coronation ceremonies, the sea repeats the sacred gesture of allegiance to the sea.
Likewise, the man against God shows his attachment to man even beyond death.

Years of flesh, of nerves, of bone. Years of blood and saliva. The soul does not age. The body is the moment.
Childhood. Old Age. The body babbles, demonstrates, surrenders.
In death, the soul finds the soul.

Of this day out of phase you keep what was never your portion of happiness, but the gears of your hate.

You have as it were come out of the falling leaves of your childhood, the garden of your intoxicating years. The past conceived your form. One moment shaped it for the next which modified it in turn. You are no more yourself today than you were yesterday. You are no more yourself than you will be tomorrow.
You pass through space as one steps over a brook, as one crosses a

river or climbs over a dune. Birds, fish, dry black scarabs are all in the book. You fly from one sky to another, swim from one river to the next, wander from desert to desert.

Your name is Yaël. You do not fear God.

You are accompanied by the child you were and the girl whose ruffled virginity wakes in her shadow like a crumpled page thrown down and picked up again in the morning at the foot of the bed, page where words of desire ride those of humiliation.

And that child dead with the world that you drag along in your eyes . . .

You are called Yaël, and you try to sew together the pieces of your name.

So young to have a name in shreds.

Child, child
with heavy braids and hooked nose.
I do not recognize your face,
but I know your eyes.

Girl, girl
with short hair and chapped lips.
I do not recognize your face,
but I know your eyes.

Woman
with the book behind your forehead, in your closed lids.
We, in our prison, decipher the pages
where beings, things, the world are written by our eyes.

I happened to imagine you as you were.
Sometimes life comes alive in the stroke of a pen.
We shall pretend we are living.

2

I know what I shall say.
I know what I shall write.
What I say will be heard,
what I write, read.
Tomorrow already defined.
Tomorrow—but where? when?

You came to surprise me in the little room of our apartment
where I often work by myself. You were naked under your peach-
colored gown. You wanted to chat. Far from your body and its gates.
Out of the pit.

I offered you cigarettes. You smoked heavily.

I was a pebble talking to water. You must not think that a stone in
the harsh sun does not suffer from thirst. Water is the hostile sister
of fire. Both are begotten by death.

Words of light withdrawn as they came, blurred shimmer of
waived claims, do I know what you said?

When you fell silent, the light was too much.

Dawn found us folded in each other's arms.

Silence: the wellspring.

I have watched you for a long time. I have long been waiting for
the hour when I shall see only what you hide from me, hear only
what you do not breathe a word about.

Where our lives rest a sealed sun hoists its fire.

Time means wear and tear, but truth is diluted in the lakes of for-
given tests. Movement takes place in the mirage, at the edge of
thirst. Up the first stairs, the first step. No more distance between
wing and verge. The path is strewn with dead birds. The desert begins where the tree loses its roots and the grass its spring.

Yaël, the door we shall knock at will be of air. Our fists will be of feathers. They will glide, birds, while once scissors of hate.

They will people the sky. And the sun will give back their shadow.

You can hardly stand the insinuating voice of things which, curving it, lets silence be mirrored in silence.

O mirror where sounds are like butterflies taking leave of the flowers.

We inhale the face.

Night reverses the image.

We are bound to one another by a kind of complicity born of our not wanting to end it. You were aware of this from the beginning.

Were you going to opt for frank deeds which would free you in regard to yourself and us? You chose the mud. Bogged down we adapt as we can.

At the surface, like two puddles of muddy water, your eyes examine space, question the dust of stars out of phase whose cries sprinkle the world.

Your youth cries vengeance for the harm you do me and weigh me down with. We are one and the same victim. So that I never know if you do not see yourself when you look at me.

In sleep your eyes are the torch which shows the crops are seized for debt. By day they threaten me like those haphazard swords with gutter sheaths which you see shimmering along the sidewalk to the sewer, or like those needles of noon whose unbearable prick even the stones remember.

In your pupils our world is peopled with birds from your islands, with tame animals. You scratch and let yourself be scratched. Your thoughts have beaks and wings.

It was your eyes, Yaël, gave you away. At the beginning they would halt halfway between you and me, as if to take a breath or to decide on their direction. This hesitation which your smile tried to mask was so awkward, you were so embarrassed that I thought you were dying with shyness.

Later the way you looked at me changed. Your eyes went through me as if you had suddenly gotten the power to make me invisible. You went through me without worrying about the wound you left. This went on for months while the seeds of solitude sprouted on our land fed by silence.

Then, one morning, your look changed again. Helpless, I watched the new metamorphosis. I saw your eyes withdraw, gather inward, focus and fuse with that knot of vegetative fever which is the flower in its first bud and whose fatal scent will, on its opening, cause death.

Was it from fear of measuring yourself against my disdain or my anger—or perhaps even my love—that you chose, that night, to take refuge in the banal pretext of a sudden migraine which froze you at a distance where I could still touch you, but where you no longer were mine?

Ruses are perfect mediators where commitment is lacking, where the soul is so upset and divided that it does not have the courage to face the verdict of reason. Then reason decides by itself, weighs the pro and contra with all the rigor of which it is capable.

In the name of a logic whose bond you are you hoist the lie to the top of the flagpole, as the deck boy does with the ship's pennons, in order to pursue your voyages far from our dull shores.

What promise of countries offers to run thrills through your indolence? You risk adventure without anybody, indifferent to all.

I have become such a burden to you that your boredom constantly clamors for something new, for unapproachable shores, for vaster oceans.

As your eyes reach out toward death, do you see there a chance to survive where I am not?

You had to kill me in what never existed, to evict me from what I never possessed, to pretend to give me what you were going to take away with a jeer.

You would triumph at this game where Nothing ploughs and re-ploughs Nothing.

At a loss when I call you, in furs when I want you naked. You attract me the better to reject me. And your eyes shine with their highest fever.

You have isolated the mouth and made it your ally without body or soul.

If the word is the great hope of the lie, then you have made the show of pleasing and loving into the mouthpiece of contradictory behavior which leads straight to my ruin. I postpone the worst. I watch you humiliating me.

What disappointed passion for truth drives you? I was so confused that for a long time I took it to be your loveliest virtue. Are we going in the same direction in our quest of the absolute? We swore we would never swerve from our course. Like me, you try to go beyond yourself into your indestructible soul. We started from the same point. At the finish, you strip a shadow while I welcome the exiled dew.

Bound with all the ropes of a savage slavery.

You spent the morning with *the other*. Did the sea speak to you its language of impatient tides? Coming back, a tear surged to the edge of your lashes. For this humble drop I will forgive for a long time.

In our tears flows the morning blood of God. Dawn became the bitter dread of His loss.

The second is framed in time as the mirrors with edges of foam are in the sea which breaks them. Water cannot hold water. So the islands remind us.

He owes you his assurance, and you submit unflinchingly, without anger, to his yoke. Glorified in a way and bruising yourself.

It is in your eyes, which distort the world they capture, that I shall punish you. I shall creep in cautiously, flat on my belly, as into a camp fenced with barbed wire. Like a hero or a criminal.

What will you do when you notice me there, deep in your pupils? How will you try to throw me out? Or will you forget about me? Then I would die the horrible death of the shipwrecked.

You pretended to be surprised when I told you I had settled in your eyes. I broke the news with a certain detachment and then took pleasure in a detailed description of the inner landscape I had discovered there. I spoke of the beach where, together with *the other*, you embraced a world of sand and sky made up by the sun. Did you not steal this part of the infinite from me? I mentioned the night when, together, you formed a heart in tune whose beat gave its rhythm to the world.

You questioned me as if you were trying to catch me out. You wanted to know what I was getting at. You wanted to know, through me, what you were getting at. Then you turned your back to me. Did I even know who you were?

The other knows your name. He can call you. Can spell you. For him you embody each of your letters, the four yardarms of your escapes. Letter differs from letter in disgrace; in daring, they form one and the same sail. Over there, in a land that eagerly awaits you, a tearful idol caps the view.

You love without love unless it is a love which crosses you out. In passing you push aside the scream. Where will you stop? You are both the prelude and the end of the voyage, both unique and a crowd whose many faces irretrievably move away yours. So that you love with inexhaustible distance.

The void leads you astray to places where you are only a sign of absence, a coming of fog white as a galaxy, as if the evening meant to join the evening by a forbidden path.

Your dead relatives (so close to you in their promise not to reproduce) are those marvels of likeness warranted by eternity in what has no longer form or function.

You are a message without mast which one can pick up like a pebble. Citizen of unreal countries, indomitable lover, you leave it to *the other* to sort out the hymns that challenge the surface image of the world.

What color gives to light is a present of transparency.

Who will contradict the claim that a black lamp inside man makes him black, a yellow lamp yellow, a white lamp white?

The sea never comes back to the sea.

Were you, that evening, on the point of giving in, carried away by a trying obsession whose deadlock roused your blood and marked your cheeks?

You got hold of yourself very fast.

Your blush turned to a strange pallor and, when I least expected it, you crushed your lips against mine.

Yaël, my mouth is still dazzled by that kiss. It blinded my throat, burned my lungs. I opened to the miracle like a tree to the fruit which would feed it. I forgot the present to remember only the logs of happiness in the fireplace without minding the heat that consumed them. I kissed your forehead, stroked your hair. One second pushed the next on to a flowered path traced in flames.

Suddenly you broke from my embrace, recoiled and burst into laughter.

You laughed a long time. This laugh was an admission of both your omnipotence and your defeat. I felt immense pity for you. I said to myself that you were bearing harm like an unmarried mother her child of scandal and misery.

Then you launched into futile remarks, but I did not listen. I heard the noise of a hammer smashing slate.

Outside, it was raining. You undressed slowly. For a moment you stood naked in front of the mirror. You did not seem to know you were undressed.

I married you, Yaël, for your independence, for that moral health I needed. Because I always had to pay for compromises.

You were twenty-five. I was a few years older. Our hands had searched for each other from road to road. So when they joined one morning I thought (and perhaps you thought also) that nothing would ever separate us.

I made you enter a world of trust and offerings where the word of truth was to come before anything. And I told you that without this word the world was to be rejected, denied.

Truth wanted to be equal to the law to whose demands our bodies and souls submitted in advance.

You said: "We shall not change the world, but we shall be one wellspring. Let the river vanish into the sea. You and I will drink out of our matched palms."

You became my refuge towards which I rowed with joy. Where you were all was pure and even ugliness absolved. Our movements were carried by our words, and we wandered through the explored space of our lips.

Why does this hate of the lie break up my life? Have I not seen how under its rule the surest mechanisms break down, strong men fall like mined walls, horizons close at the threshold of the infinite? Have I not seen how fire breaks the faith of humble but noble plots of land, how the night erases even the memory of dawn's good-bye? Before I met you, being born seemed cheating. So many victims in the name of an idea of man and God throw their shadow over the page where I claim you. So many lands, so many things, so many leaves show me their wounds where the syllables call for me.

Yaël, you were my consolation and support. My pen learned, paragraph by paragraph, to close in on the truth of a vocation always challenged and called into question. It secured the right to share in the fruit of hunger, having paid its tithe. It claimed the privilege, in the name of radiant love, to nestle against words and margins of the book like a lover against the breasts of his beloved.

Two of us to challenge the Powers of darkness which deflected the natural course of events. We stayed aloof in our perseverance, forcing river and rain to flow around the witness-rock we were. Two of us inside existence and outside time where the hour banished us. A bond had been formed between country and childhood. The trees lived the epic of wood, and insects invented their thirst.

You preferred birds to flowers because, you told me, when they fly they have no shadow. As if there were neither evening nor morning.

Truth wanted to be so simple for you that I thought my work as a writer was born of the spontaneity of one of your familiar gestures. I touched the roots. Branches opening out into leaves seemed as obvious to me as man fulfilling himself.

Sap spurted from sap. We were our own seasons and the giddy will to obey sun and rain.

Was I so anxious about my salvation that I neglected to watch you? This happens to people consumed with a fire of ore.

To die of dying in part. We shall support each other in the changes we impose on the knowing hour.

Even absence needs a center. You are in it. You let the world turn around, turn in vain to the point of twisting.

To what need to subvert the natural order of things can we chalk it up that most of us support absence and are its partisans?

To what lawful death can we oppose an extravagant voluntary death bred by violence?

We answer with a thousand vast murmurs, with a deaf hum of mother-of-pearl which the ocean disputes with every wave.

To die with every gesture that gives way to a new gesture. Had I, in front of the chance page, abused the sky like you?

To be a word, to accept denying myself for a word.

Hence I assumed an arbitrary future of absence which hid me from myself.

Hence, unable to give an authoritative sense to my life, I bargained with the void at the heart of the word.

This nonexistent center became the favorite place of my pen, the well of dark where the words came to drink before dying on the page. Thus books complete themselves in the book. When I am alone my voice turns to ink. Who ever knows where we are.

Talk was yours by right. It made you extravagant within the word. You were shameless in your vice.

But once outside words you settled in the modest dignity of the insulted wife.

Your ambition, however, remained boundless, a scrupulous megalomania.

The writer's art owes you its best showing. Are you not the quarry of the words we hold up?

Yaël, when I, at the end of my pains, denounced writing as a God-given and God-begetting lie because it is loyal to the claims of the signs, I was floundering between two expressions of one truth lived in relation to a vast reality. So that the word changed nothing, but interpreted things with a name, in terms of an image, a sound. The object remained out of reach even when grasped, when shown in its failure to show.

Then I said to myself that I had perhaps half-opened the soul of things with my words—which were now their soul—and had anticipated their future in their blossoming dreams.

To feel means to approach the pain or joy of the world.

Will I always be what I see or touch and never myself in my own buoyant energy?

If human truth is lack of ties—a lake to mirror yourself or drown— it is also the fateful encounter of two beings like that of the world and the word.

Faced with a thing, truth lies in the feeling which soon rejects it. Even if it spread the infinite from all the windows we would make our fortune by losing it.

Poverty is its condition: a seed, a grain of sand. Be it sterile or fruitful, truth dies of sterility or fruitfulness. Our lot is to interpret an unreadable world.

Who are you, Yaël, to cheat against yourself the person you want to be? What insane god furled your senses so prematurely that you cannot stand the world with its fogs and its colors?

Night favors the alliance of Good and Evil with an even coolness of the woods.

You are the excuse for crime, the preamble to the conversation of hangman and victim.

A stranger to the crystal which stirs the fragrant sail of the void among the waves, you tell the beads of the iodine-tinted hour, closed curve escaped from the shore. O longing born of the perverse deep sea of the mind and the senses.

A buried world answers for you. *The other* polishes the marble slab where you engraved your greenhouse breasts.

Gorgeous in your serene assurance where earth and sky share the same night of shipwreck.

Dwelling a little on the plausible motives of your doings I was led to conclude that your skill in baffling the decree of day within the light itself depended on your never facing it. You approached the light obliquely, looked in its farthest nooks for means to discourage its being alive.

A deceased light would allow you to build on its ruins: palaces and prisons, careful guardians of your glory. The broken lamp keeps the blaze of its nightly dominion.

You were able to celebrate the morning, but only through the sky. There was always the interval of a world between us.

More than once did I hope to cross the space where dreams accompany the signs, where writing whispers promises of ports. Over there, at the end of my waiting, you would have been mine like those phonemes caught in ink, visibly mine even down to your soul.

Who are you, Yaël, to scorn the rescue which I lit up with the moment?

The night lent you its silken net, and you fished an unknown fauna and flora in the swelling flood. Did *the other* praise the beauty of his realm? He as it were read in you because you are both world and word.

Together you sealed the folds of the deep which no ray of light disturbs. Liquid night in its monstrous memory.

Who are you, Yaël, to prefer your uncreated face to the one I am patiently modeling? You are and you are not this woman whom her mirror drives back to her longing to be.

You have no handle to your eyes. Let those whom you seduce carry you off. Pure resemblance does not belong to anything. The lace of salty dark adorns the earth, and the universe rises from oceanic shadows.

Your mirror is the padded abyss where your eyes, which nothing else can hold, dive in. Reality hammered by your distrust takes shape at the outset of an adventure without audience. To reestablish silence in the din of exposed existence. To be the lead that weights the line.

Of all the women who free you, which has your characteristic self-consciousness? Which has so violent a taste for victory in imposture that nothing can distract her from her role?

I came home later than usual. You were writing. Your pad of blue paper was on the table, and near your elbow were several sheets scored with your delicate handwriting which I loved for all it used to let me guess.

I knew you were writing to *the other*. But what could you have to say to him? Did you not meet him every day? Were you sending him your last missive?

You put the pages in the envelope without rereading them. You turned to me and said: "What time is it? I'll be ready to go out in a moment."

I replied there was no need to hurry, we had all the time. And this sentence immediately blurred because my anxiety loaded it with fog and addressed it to the night. My eyes met yours. It was clear they would be the last to die.

I must have looked at you sadly, because you felt the need to add: "I was writing to my mother."

I knew you were lying. You were wise enough not to insist. I did not ask any questions. I let you crawl like a reptile in its poison.

The hours we then spent with your guests in your favorite noisy night club on the Right Bank are tied to the quick moment when you slid your letter into your lover's pocket.

I had left our table to speak to an old friend I had noticed—but it was really a pretext. I am out of sympathy with your friends, knowing how much they know about us. A pillar was between us. You thought no doubt that I could not see you. When I came back you wanted to dance. Once on the floor you pressed close to my body. I shut my eyes hoping to spill all the ink in the world over the miserable hashed-up images that obsessed me. Your body swept mine along. We were a boat full of music rocked by the waves. Suddenly I heard you say so privately that every word could have been a secret caress for heart and ear: "Remind me to mail my letter tomorrow morning. You know how I forget."

Is this how ships are wrecked? The wave is loyal to the wave. No one can ever break the chains of water.

Within reach of our paired lances, who will help us in our blindness? You know what morass at the threshold of love stings my eyes. The battles we fight are wars of the dark, of two against one. You deliberately change camps, and this back-and-forth smothers even the hardiest root of day.

I cling to the rock. I must win. At whatever cost.

I accept my truth now as a gift, now as my due.

I sound out the sun in its beds of knowledge, in its craters of beliefs where ink is sister to lava.

Unlike those heroines, those mistresses of their fate who entered history by ruse, you do not have full power. You are not free to dismiss me (though I thought so for a long time). You are bound to respect the rules of the game. You must strike your blows of dagger and diamonds in daylight.

(Witches and fairies are said to wear their weeping and weapons on their fingers. Mystery of rings. Secret ambitions of jewels sorted out by death.)

I stubbornly try to reconstruct the shelter of fresh leaves which will set us apart in the seed. The ground does not cut us off from the heart of the earth. Unity is in the kernel we keep, as it is in the named pulp.

My short, because frequent, forays into the light will no longer resemble the take-off of the flying fish subdued by the sky nor the raids of rats writhing with hunger.

Day will be my archipelago. My house will meet the sea. Pebbles will fill my hands. I shall be protected.

Written, my life will be reborn from its ruin. Thus fruitful land at the foot of the volcano keeps the indomitable farmers.

This late afternoon I watch how all around me the flowers and trees get heavy along with the walls that are given back to themselves. And I think of the effort the earth will have to make tomorrow to shake off the weight of its absence.

Yaël, what energy is yours? Heavy—heavier than the planet—with a life made to vanish in the freshest morning of its course.

Except for you, everything is false in the word that confounds us.

Thus the mask wins out over the face wherever the day surrenders.

In the winter of idylls I am a fireplace knocked about by the wind, a hearth of daring ruled by a long meditation of fire whose force undoes the cold of an existence doubled over on itself and already old with its life.

Once I was mistaken enough to compare a fireplace to the dawn of happiness. Are commentaries burned under the poker not like those evenings when words find no taker, nor do hands?

Death is the continued lack of passion which thought and word maintain. In its original truth the world is thus without face. Tomorrow memory will rage and the universe again take form in man's mind and the raised planes of his soul. The star will consume the star whose every twinkle is a blink of memory. Memory ripens with the dawn. Lie which turns away from the moment when God recognized Himself in the silence from the far side of a light which day keeps from our eyes. For God stopped seeing in order not to be seen.

You would live in the secret of a separation of which you are breath and shoot. But your calls never clear the horizon.

You announced your decision to put a partition up in our bed-room. The room is enormous. We shall each have a place which will depersonalize us. We shall meet on waking like two strangers having gone through the night.

You insisted it was urgent to give up a habit you called unhealthy. You drew your lessons from convincing examples.

"One day," you added, "we would have hated each other."

Your death cannot be an easy one. The kind which attracts you asserts itself in fire. A filtered ray of moonlight.

A wall, I thought, between two people hitting it with their fists.

I forgot that space quarters a dwelling.

I watch the world become mute where the wings of the word are clipped. Bird song is a voluptuous gliding with complicated patterns in the flat grey of its moan, with delicate lines and large blossoms mixed into its green unconcern.

First, my relations with *the other*. It began with Yaël suddenly turning her eyes from their object to take in a world where I was not, a world ruled by a Prince whose lack of name added to the plea-sure of giving him one.

Yaël went towards him. Happy. Did she find again old faded steps of hers or that long call which had become so weak with failing that one day it turned from cry into sob and finally dried up?

On coming back, she asked me:

"Had you already met him?"

"Perhaps," I replied and walked away.

Was he not like the one whom she described to me in her shame-less whisper?

He tried, with his arm over his face, to shield his eyes from the stabbing rays of the sun. Dark glasses were not enough.

You stretched out next to him. He turned his back to the light. There was so much darkness in you, Yaël, that he felt safe beside you. No longer afraid of the sky. You were his sky and every sensitive particle of your being sparkled for him like those clues of evening we call stars.

A morbid love joins night to the earth. You were a daughter of night before you gave in to the day. I should have known it by your difficulty to break from that unquenchable presence you often summoned in silence and which veiled your eyes. Long daydreams from which you returned changed. I payed no heed, putting it down to a legitimate longing for deserted banks besieged by waves. You were so young in your hurt flesh that ebbing pleasure must have left deep washes of algae and bitter kisses.

You had barely outgrown adolescence when you had your first experience of night. You sacrificed your phosphorescent body. Your sex branched out, and you took pleasure in the whole expanse of your glow. You told me this. Responding to my desire you seemed slowly to leave the place your virginity had stained with drops of something more than blood for the bed of thorns which the sun has bequeathed to us.

Lying between us you could face our fates. The light reduced me to myself. The dark adorned him with the prestige of the elect.

In his flattered strength he was the lucid moment of a precarious arrangement in which death joined.

Mirrors die the death of the lynx in a spared look. The world endures in the landscapes we remember while we live. The light of love is that of drunk retinas, its hurt dark that of lowered lids.

You keep your eyes open at night. A wound which will never scar over speaks terror through your sleep:

"I am Yaël. I take what I want. I give what rebuffs.

"All I care for: to live the absence of God.

"God went into exile and left it to man to unseal the world. I shall be all the lies of God in order to die of His death.

"For God died of lying. All that *exists* lies. To be in the truth means wanting Not-To-Be. God is Truth. Thus God is Union, God is Convergence."

The carnival was in full swing: a miniature world swept by movement.

A mob crowded around, eager to keep up an illusion of being alive which life itself thwarted. Diving, revolving. Gliding and rolling.

People seemed to surface out of white sheets which music and laughter pushed farther and farther off, out of a once liquid plane, a layer of paint so thin that a breeze could lift it. Space is studded with milky lakes like this. You see them clearly at nightfall when the air is all slowness and the hour dense. Lakes of immemorial time, isolated and cold, with only the shape of a lake left, but where the instant still comes to drown with the stars.

How did they become so small? A rose stripped of its petals in a frenzy. So the starry night took on the dimensions of man's fears and rest: a feast of death and life joined on earth.

Suddenly, as we left the tunnels of horrors to let the militant mirrors distort us whose obsession with the ugly leads to the wildest follies, you said to me: "Is this you?" Entering into your game I replied: "No." Then you threw yourself screaming into the arms of *the other*: "He's changing. He's forced to change too. It's not him. It's you."

The other violently pushed you away. Later he apologized and put his gesture down to momentary excitement. I looked into your eyes. There was in them, there was, there was all the slapped pride of centuries without God.

Journal II

Dusk has the skin of an old man. Chiseled by the once-famous rays.

That uneasy position of star on fire and star of water.
Neither here nor there.
The sun has the attention of the sand.

Venus's flytrap. She eats souls.

The plant turned shooting star surprises the man who is awake late.

Light of the great trees of hunger, with saw-toothed leaves.
You cannot contemplate the celestial body.

You taught me to appreciate the velvet paths of a countertruth for which you took vows.

Your actions took on significance as they carried out the sentence pronounced by the titled voices of an implacable justice vexed by certainty. Justice of wise men and God, likewise Satan's justice.
It was your lot to be lost in a world not made on your scale. A world black and glistening like shot

silk where the individual is betrayed by the universe and man.

God's contradictions are the contradictions of truth.

Wanting to be true you run the risk of never being so. Instants of truth: stake of absence.

Ah, until our death the lie will be the pink sandstone we dig with our angles and the straw on which we burn.

You cannot free salt from its thirst.
Here even the Prince loses his privilege.

Cut in two. Which is mine?
The two halves of a fruit are equally tasty.

Knowing disillusioned your steps. You prefer *the other*.

Blood in its veins: a melody of mirrors.

Assonance. An echo is a way station of our wanderings, a chance of the hooked word.

Let every sound be the radiant summer of a step.

Words migrate like birds suddenly turned strangers in their sky, like men in their homes.

I have often asked myself from what horizons they came. Sensitive to the seasons they dream of sunny regions which need not be regions of harsh light. There are stars—like the kind of quartz called cat's-eye—that are more beautiful than the star of noon for having contained their fire and been careful of their reflection. Their dream is always action.

Knots: eyes sleeping, growing. The tree becomes what it sees.

Water lights up the eyes.

O Yaël, tireless voyage across the lie of oceans, your belly and haunches are the moist shores of desire, your breasts two horizons caught in the skin. You will founder, too sure of the stuff you are made of, too sure it will float.

I am heavy. Your body is under mine.

We are sinking, Yaël. After you I shall take my last deep breath. I shall keep all the warm air of earth and sky one moment longer in my lungs. One moment, Yaël: the time of the book.

I had given up this journal for the time being. I cannot claim I put it out of my mind.

I prowled around, unable to take up the pen. We were suddenly incompatible—an inexplicable situation like death fighting the memory of death.

This trip to Les Landes, facing the unleashed ocean, the wind and its constant impious onslaught on the world, has only made matters worse.

Spectral condors swelling the mad dreams of the sea, who can say which threat is more ominous, that of night or that of day? The stones did not breathe. Our eyes sunk deeper into our faces, so heavily did the salt-laden air and the dark stick to the skin.

Yaël, you were shut out from my journal. I watched you go about, leave and come back to *the other* or me, sometimes—often—to both of us. Your voice was neutral. Your manner unchanged. But the landscape had become so real that it alone could be heard, that it was visibly unique.

The whole universe flowed onto this shore, existed only for it and its austerity at the heart of silence.

The ocean gave us our daily quota of jewels. At low tide we went and took possession. It made us see the tracks of the lie in every shell which you pierced and strung on a thread with other shells, the lie whose history is that of the sea.

One day you put the string around your neck, and I retraced without you, but for both of us, the intimate, tangled path of our seasons of blood.

What is rebellion but the ripening of the lie? Excess eggs it on. Foam that the ocean spills, froth in which it washes and grinds. So much blood no sooner formed than lost, but recovered in the breakers. So much blood sacrificed to the exasperating riot of the water.

For hours on end I stared at the flood of our gestures cramped in their space as the most lavish spectacle of pain and horror unfolded, the worse for the terrified silence of the earth.

I was the ground and its restrained trembling, its wet face, its beaten look.

Yaël, life was there, right in front of us, with its possessive past and forecast future. Our bustling is vain where it is only the dizziness of bewildered wings.

Thus events move and sacrifice us to their own momentum. The hour bears witness to an intuition of our acts which it knows to keep on a leash.

Shall we be unprotected on the last voyage our prow carries us?

You will not hide your forehead in your arms folded around their flesh. Water does not shield a body covered with tears. Night is with us in the boat and shipwreck lies in wait.

Yaël, we shall be rain, broken by our defeats. Our mouths salty at the edge of the foggy abyss.

On the beach, your toe had dug up a dead fish. You said to me: "If you overcame your disgust and decided to eat it you would be poisoned. So it is with truth." And you added: "Nakedness is the first stage of death. Take me naked. Eternity will deliver me of my flesh."

And yet, the fear of vanishing, the dread of being smoothed out—for is form not the courage of curves?—misgivings as to reality which is a lack of reality, i.e., a passive lack, the kind which mopes in its lack—these anxieties, these fears you had to the point of panic and no doubt from the moment when you gave birth to an inert child, to a dumb hope for syllables covered with a bit of flesh.

Nobody can checkmate death.

For the first time, I questioned myself where you did not dare intervene. It was as if you were suddenly stricken with silence in order to isolate, within our tortured history, a question left unformulated because the answer did not concern you.

I bet on myself, on my passion for life which I had transferred onto you in the love you had kindled.

I bet outside any possible surrender where you lord it waiting for a sign of stifled yearning which you alone could revive.

I bet crowded in an enclave of bleak light where dusk was a haven.

My foot caught in the trap of the moment. A scared visitor where the fire will soon reach the grain elevators of night. Will I not go on? From heel to forehead, I am a block of blue sky.

No sooner is a sentence composed than it is flooded.

Where the ocean groans, the book perishes by the book. Could it be that the word of truth has drowned? In that case, hero of the dive, your death would be that of the world.

The other has left us for a week in Spain. We shall wait for him here and go back to Paris with him, in his car.

From her bedroom, Yaël calmly watched him leave.

Yaël said: "Truth opens onto itself. We shall go into the void of truth like a blind demiurge."

How long have I held a grudge against you for the vagueness you cultivated with subtle calculation? It left you without alliance in the labyrinths of your hasty conclusions, as if our features no longer showed up in the light and we could be interchanged with impunity, forgetting ourselves and the world, as if the universe suddenly crumbled with the face to serve as posthumous preface to nothingness?

Death is glorious modeling clay for the artist. It will be admired or despised accordingly. Likewise the clay sculpture which, buried in the ground, prefigures man.

Likewise with us, Yaël, at the heart of creation. But if I kick or snort, your work, even though fastened to its pedestal, will smash on its shadow on the ground.

You are hostile towards me as you are towards all that you have not created.

You only accept what comes from yourself. You only take what your own hands offer.

You love *the other*, not for himself, but against me.

The water's pain makes the wind groan.

Yaël could not bear the separation she had agreed to. I had the feeling she had let *the other* go off in her sleep without taking him from her dream. Or was it me who was asleep and dreaming?

Could he only talk about himself to her when she begged that he talk about her?

Porous world, blood oozes out everywhere. O seeds of the most solemn oath.

The agave stem is a feast of misfortune. And it revels in the end of day.

Beautiful gate to the secret of wounds.

Everything is in the book, and God is its lightness.

Giving to read means rising, lighter and lighter, up into the Totality. It also means suppressing yourself where the word is read.

The sky empties the sky.

The sea swallows the sea.

The earth covers the earth.

Your body is an empire periodically rebuilt. Your eyes take hold of mine, and I imagine.

Between me and me, Yaël cannot choose.

She tears into my two painted portraits.

The painter lied.

Yaël, who is this artist with a brush more gossipy than your need to plead not guilty each time you appear?

You applaud him where I lose my footing.

Unfeasible absence.

O windows of sleeping glass, sleep holds golden immensities. And night agrees.

What love potion will give you hope for a short-winded dawn? Greyness guards our shores.

Uneasy pregnancy of the globe. The days form a circle above the clouds in order to hand around the sun.

Here, flight means a sham upright position with raised arms. Andriagas champ at the cloud-gate.

You live. You win. Farewells share the fate of the gods.

Yesterday I got back to my room, my things, my books.

I sat down at my worktable and copied the pages brought back from Les Landes into my journal. Without dating them. What for?

Vacation. The time responsible for our wrinkles held in check by our dreams. No counting. No measuring. But watch out for the awakening. The hour does not abdicate.

Death is a long curtain between us, a hanging which blood cannot stain. It is evenly red, as red as a body torn open just before the end.

This idea I held of death was quickly borne in upon me.

Idea with a double edge. I kill and die, haunted by its serene mark.

The world does not answer to its name or, rather, shows its forgotten side. The sea is the reverse of the sea, and the earth has its earlier features, the miraculous roundness of the beginning.

I read the words of death. Eye that bears fruit, latent eye. The tree dwells on the past of the tree.

Let the world live by its vanquished violence. Let it prosper in its dark guts.

The milestone will always be of stone. But the wave, the shadow: who could think of fixing them?

Leaving without leaving. Stubborn thirst.

Do not water the anchor. It leads the life of an intruder. The sea rusts and erodes its iron.

Fusion in death allows for the most absurd speculations on the future of the face and its gestation. Thus I resemble you, and together we are different from the separate creatures we were. A mixture of you and me—man or woman?—takes our place. I have your hair, and you find your nose as you look at mine. You have my mouth and my forehead whereas my neck has grown longer and thin to become yours.

When the light dims we grow pale with it. We keep our bodies, but no longer have any purpose.

Yaël and I, joined as we never were before, at the expense of our cheated individualities which love had bullied into choosing one another.

We went beyond what is natural. We opened an era of uncertainty whose eyes reduced to blindness will pay for it.

We shall take up the dream of roots.

A trench. We crawl, heads close to the ground. Thus creeping shadows sniff each sprout of the cautious plant and its hidden motives.

But higher Yaël, higher up, there is the abrogating emptiness within us.

O floodgates of time in its fullness.

From my chair I am watching a bird search through the bereaved morning for the kindness of the world.

Safe from reversals.

It is freezing in our hearts. Ice block. Ice block.

That evening, I listened to Yaël describing our vacation to her friends in our living room.

Exercises on the beach on getting up. Swimming till noon: "Knocked about by the waves—they came as high as nine feet. We were put down and laughed at endlessly."

After lunch, we would take the car to Biarritz, Saint-Jean-de-Luz, Ascain.

At Hossegor, "chistera" parties. And that bullfight which made us go to Bayonne. A bullfight so popular because of one famous matador that even beforehand the fear and excitement spiraled off into unfathomable depths.

In the arena, the fight of death against death, its double representations, human and animal, opposed for an instant in the cruelest ballet this side of the grave.

In a circle, above, sickles of fanatic flames, screams cut off, burned: an audience of arsonists spreading fire with their eyes.

Moments of truth, of which memory keeps the image of weird wounds, as of a flag shredded by the winds and fire of a universe at stake.

Canvas of pain. Embroidery soon spattered with its rose windows of red spears and swords.

Banality of last days. Is there a new kind of chain for criminals' eyes? Not a blindfold, but real irons to rivet the pupils to the bruised ground, to the rotten roots?

So the flower chaffs the flower, and the blade of grass the butterfly.

Every creature is allotted an acre of void to settle in.

In human terms, does this mean entering into the possession of a vital space? But the most fortunate will never come to own theirs.

The infinite is property of death.

We speak to others, to the enemies of personal statements, in order to open our words to their own plurality.

Agreement and refusal are the arches and turns of discourse.

Man has always died on the road.

A rule of life. Every law is consistent within itself. We want laws to be just so that we can unveil their spirit and submit to it of our own will.

Faith offers its face to the law.

Let this face be of granite, Yaël.

Mountains are the monstrous sight of screams stifled by the earth.

Journal III

Silence helps secrets.

The silence between object and object: the distance man takes from man, and shore from shore.

In the unfolded wings of silence, unexplored worlds spread their solitude.
Ruthless religion of trees. The top hears only the top.
The time of questioning is a time of help. Every request tastes of almonds.

Learning to talk, a child little by little leaves the book which the night had let him leaf through.
A mystery is perhaps only an after-word which fuses with the easily undone knots against which the void rebels. A knot like a pause of the mind in its coupling plunge.
Thus the word masters its movements.

Could it be that the dark is the inner movement of words? But truth is not verbal. It is the place words come back to at night.

You have set up a dialogue between you and yourself, a dialogue of creator and creature, in the course of which you succumb to your own voice.

We are closer to one another than to ourselves.

Believing is the only possible way of being.

Space has passed the deal, and it is only the measure of a named world.

The ultimate face is a universe.

1

A man called death a tide:
life sings
at high tide; at low tide
the world weeps.

A man called death a bride:
life sings
on the wedding day; in the night of man
the world weeps.

A man called death a canopy:
the iris sings
under blue sky; in the dark of walls
the world weeps.

A man called death like himself:
the body sings
with all pores at dawn; at dusk
the soul weeps.

This man, where is he?
Death is calling.

2

Let us take our bearings. Let us see.

To be myself in *the other*. Graph of our route till now. Yaël, the feminine half of a being that does not say where it is going. So it is with the plant once out of the ground. We think it is rooted to its life because it seems so obedient to its set form. But the plant grows against the plant. It worries about likeness. Particular trees. Conspicuous flowers. Never the same. Sleep makes them bloom, and the day kills them.

No wound is like another. Branches and stems bleed for themselves alone.

Monotonous lie. Digression greying out. Imagining is now only a degrading abdication before the sovereign intact face of the millennia.

Supremacy of nature. The earth throws us back to the last image.

The earliest order is that of death. Divine order backed by all that is eternal in the creature.

Third season, season of dealing with death.
Fall with shades of waning ochre.
Days pass. Centuries fritter away.

I am trying to explain to myself why *the other* had such influence over us from the beginning. I think if I could find out why we both took such interest in him or even just fix the day and hour when he came into our lives I would come to understand the way we acted toward him. For I did nothing to turn you from him.

Does he embody the heart's stubborn resistance against the sick equivocations of desire?

Royal heart, profoundly loyal. With eulogies for logic.

Have you ever left him since your first adolescent turmoil? Was it always he following you wherever you thought you were going?

Did you disown him when you met me?

There are evenings when I ask myself whether we did not pull him out of those borderline regions we like to skirt and whether we will not die of it.

He was who I would have liked to be and whom you would have liked to be with.

So we have lived in *the other*'s anxiety.

One through the one.

One without the one.

I remember the morning on a mountain path when we met a blond man of medium height, with a high forehead and such wonder in his eyes that we would have sworn that he was discovering the marvels of things and of the world. A foreigner probably. He smiled at us, and we politely smiled back.

He impressed us very much. You did not talk about him, but his image froze between us and slowly forced itself on us, O solid death, as our third face.

The other's rigidity made every step dangerous. His complexity will be a face revoked by the face.

You are a glutton for life you have given breath to. You love him for our death.

The other saved in death by Yaël. And she herself saved through him. The void comes to the aid of the void. *The other* fell in with a preconceived pattern; this is what makes him, all by himself, *the other*.

I hang on to his coattails. Trying to follow I sometimes pass him, sometimes go beyond your gesture, Yaël. Then I upset you. Then I hull a profusion of thoughts.

For a moment, your face is engulfed in mine.

He knocks at my door. Discreetly. He comes in. He stands there without budging. Silent.

It is then I see all the way down into your soul, as if your love for him half opened you.

It is not you, Yaël, will wave a knife about. In your light, *the other* is a sorry, uninhabitable planet.

When you came in I murmured: "Well?"
You said: "The heart resists."
How could he live without his head? Did I not cut it off?

You asked me: "What did you do with my face?" as you might ask: "Have you seen my lipstick?"

To give a body to the dark and regret it. The body thrown to the sharks. Dark lies over the waters.

By the body you recognized him and mistook me.
Which proves that the body, before the soul, tallies with absence.
Visible in order not to be.

Does going toward what is real not mean finding unreality?

Reality is certainty of an unreality which makes us conscious of ourselves and our actions.
(Unreality of sense and fact, of sign and sanction.)
Death, a broken autumn.

He has never lived with his head. This is his head, my head: an oval, before it stretches into an olive in the void, into a stream of oil, into a fervent thread and ceases to be, but still seems to stretch further, like a ray of sunlight caught at dusk which you take with you through the night when you no longer see it, when it has already been hours that you no longer see it.
His head is not part of his body. His body stops at the neck, with

a spare head within reach. His body is not part of his being. His shoulders are not his, nor his arms. Nor his chest, pelvis, legs. An unattached being, deprived of flesh and bones. A being in the shadow of a body, of a head, of my head.

When did I kill him?
Did he kill himself?
Could I be dead also?
Done out of my revenge?
Bring him back to life. We have a score to settle. Life is balancing its books. The good accounts are endorsed by life.

Bring him back to life, Yaël.
When hurt, love relies on death.

I have, in daydreams, taken a bird's-eye view of the various forms of life. The life of an ant is not like that of man. Straight line: life of saint and hero. Zigzag line: life of the ant.
A life of light is circular, a life of water made of furrows.
What is the form of our lives, Yaël? Ants without purpose, crickets without light.
We do not even have our choice of dark
or curve.

Pyramid of rays whose tip moves with the day. The sun inside.
O tomb of the soul.
Sign dies within sign, and man within man.

Straight. We must make straight for the bank. In between, water. Woe if you cannot swim. No help for you, no herb.
Bitter herb, are you still a plant? Acid source, missing moan in the hem of light?
Birds have annexed the sky.

I walk. The earth gives way to the wings in a hurry to take all their time of travel from the air.

Where shall I stop, Yaël? I must go, go, go till the All dissolves into Nothing.

Does the book heal? That book is always to come.

Is it not strange, this book which survives death and is made of all our deaths, as if the death of a human being were only a wound which only we succumb to?

You will die in the book where I am dying
with *the other*, after God.

Ah, to die of the death of miracles.

3

This tiny thing which is a yet smaller thing
within the smallest, is that truth? Is that God?

Death unfurls the sails of recovery. The word, a consecrated healer?

Is the book as old as the soul?

Could the soul be silence inlaid with recollections? Undying memory, written forever.

Book, the best place to barter the world. Everything is infinitely different and wants to be strangely real.

The breath our bodies depend on is a clover of wind. Do we find it in the sky, the blue lawn, before the storm, or scorched by the sun?

Look what can happen to a book. The words we can no longer make out are the most important: nightly glow, ivy at dawn.

To come back to the soul: if it is a book, it is the virgin page, a sheet escaped from the pulp, the classical format of a sheet of warm air.

Life begs there for words, those birds of prey, to help it to die.

Does surviving mean living *on* life, living on a dead life, living death all life long?

Why this obsession with the book where the void wins every fight?

Why these pages like opium wounds in body and space? Why this intoxication deeper and grainier with every lost day?

Why these eyes without reading, but always ready to read? This mad will to be healed by the word when all sentences are only hiccups, shivers, sorry tics of the void?

If the creature of the dark were deprived of books he would fall back on the waste sheets.

Starry sky. Rare in this season. What does the icy fire of stars unveil? What would it transmit? This: The Light of God is exploded into space. In the night of man, every star houses an abolished gesture. But the countless writings from one frontier to another, ah, how many skies we shall never read.

I am hounding a dead God. Why go to the trouble? Death watchfully approaches death. I shall not arrive before. I cannot do better.

Tomorrow is always the day after a shadow.

To make yourself true—Truth? The mother torn asunder at the moment of birth, the creature in the instant of death.—To go on to the corrosive appraisal of the void. No quest of truth is possible outside yourself.

The lie shelters a truth eaten by its own torment.

Inside, in the guts, the decisions are made. The All voids itself. The void frays the Nothing.

I am thinking of the St.-John's-wort, that healing plant whose countless holes make me suppose now that it can cure thanks to its blatant openings onto the void.

Our recollections were our seeds.

Truth visits us, and we count its footprints which the instant, the hour, all our senses and every pulse beat of our blood pick up.

I shall have sacrificed construction to the terror of tracks.

Backing away I praise time raked out. Unaware that the reviving of its flames is one of the many revelations of solitude and death.

(Yaël, I only want to remember what hardly brushed against the dark. Your hand in mine like an imperceptible monody. O sweetness wary like the light filtered through shades.)

Arbitrary relations are repugnant to truth. Communication is an understanding based on mutual allegiance to the silence of a word at the end of lost wagers.

I have filled the books I put my name on with letters which become disappointing as they confront the truth of the void.

I have gone as far as to imagine their power as ultimate presence which fixes the beginnings of the world and its creatures and sits in judgment.

Could it be that the beginning is only an exaltation of self-denial to the point where God repents seeing the creation which consecrates His nothing?

Vanity of wombs.

And you, Yaël, who often made me cry and often were the moist jetty where my joys unfurled, what are you if not the elsewhere of a body left on deposit with those who cannot follow you?

The sea, Yaël, O monotonous murmur of our march from shore to shore.

Now I am sure of it: after its spectacular victory in the very wreck of its unity, the world will be destroyed by the world as man is every night by man.

If truth, when simply evoked, can be the victim of miscalculations, then the man of truth is the martyr of his vacant voice.
How great our misery in its confounding relations.
O Yaël, how slowly the day, each day, moves along the day.
We shall be silent on the pure page which no pen could invest.

The hour will strike. All these cruelties will stop plunging their blades into my soul and my flesh. I shall find myself without you at the end of our common suffering which the new buds upset.
To reopen life and scrape its bottom.
Lead holds the key to our dives.

Our grains of rice are half black and half white.
As we went on the black became less black, the white less white.

> Since the beginning,
> a second,
> the same one,
> ours.
> Within this second,
> day and night,
> a life,
> all life,
> and the void.

The void? A contentious point of the dark where the world forms in the dust of vanished worlds.

Where all is said.
Night speaks.

So everything happens in the silence of a word left bare.
Between two pages.

No one will be invited to this end game.

How can we accept what has all the chances to prevail, and not bother about what takes refuge in hopes?
What we shall never find is perhaps the good.

You went before me on the road, Yaël. You knew we are never done with going on in vain. You knew that the lie makes the world turn as the wind the windmill.
Reason told you to take a rest. But death is an adventuress with the sweet voice of a siren.

Your belly brought forth a storm, Yaël. Your dead child is thunder amid your tears.

"The conquest of the echo," you said, "that's what we are all after.
"The echo, shadow of a shadow, sound of an infinite of sounds, is reality, is our daily lie."

O Yaël, priestess at the Temple threshold, will you die in the odor of sanctity, a victim of the moon, a victim of your lucidity?

The All remains our wild desire for All.

The Book

If there were no more earth or sky there would still be us in the naked years we keep.

You never lose the book: you lose yourself.

I have not left my apartment. What day is it? It hardly matters. I have reread the pages written after my crime. I reread my journal as well as some sheets I had kept (since when?) in the same box. Mechanically I put them in order on top of the story of my crime and of my journal. Thus I gave birth to the book which I had composed without noticing, I mean without actually thinking of it in the course of these months outside the book.

The book does not need man to come into being. It does so through him. As in our lives we are forever pushed by the hours, one after the other. A book which could have held all the words for our thoughts and gestures, but which definitely kept only those it chose to make common cause with in their order and economy.

No way, therefore, to develop certain sentences, to add others which might have turned them from the tendency toward aphorism they so often give in to. They refused, strengthened in their attitude by a lofty idea of the book within the book, as if their concision, their proud contraction housed the light which lights up the work from within.

The book had the ambition to be the book of the eyes.

Beings and things exist only in the mirrors which copy them. We are countless crystal facets where the world is reflected and drives us back to our own reflections, so that we can know ourselves only through the universe and what little it retains of us.

The knowledge we have of ourselves rests on the interpretation of an earlier interpretation which we confirm on awaking and which precedes us into death whose instant will relate our stages across the nights.

Were the eight months before my crime only months of writing? And what is the mystery of this book which I have led to its conclusion at the price of the life of an imaginary being who was my reason to live? But is it only these eight months of pain and anxiety? Was this book not conceived earlier, much earlier? In that case everything had to happen as it did for the book. In that case I have been the instrument of an inexorable fate which the words made me take on myself.

I think of the book, and Yaël is no more. Did she die before she was born like the child of her first love? Then she and I never left the invisible kingdom of the dead where we got lost thinking we were going our ways, I in search of her, she in her desire for *the other.*

What does it matter now if she was murdered or not? Death does not have the sense we give it in death. A violent death is tied to the healthiest and worthiest act of truth. It is a dawn which all the scattered and lost shadows come to salute with a red gesture faithful to fire.

"You are a storyteller," a friend said to me one day.

How can I be when words and images always cut in and want to be heard with their own aura, when the story is built out of bits of counter-stories, and when silence lies in wait for the world?

ELYA

THE BOOK OF QUESTIONS
VOLUME V

for Gabriel Bounoure

In back of the book there is the ground of the book. In back of the ground there is immense space and, hidden in this immense space, the book we are going to write in its enigmatic sequence.

Everything is before Everything. The word is the day after the word, and the book the day after the book.

So that we turn forever around what was and will be and which, in the image of God's proud absence, stays what is, namely: the mysterious tie to the universe and the place where this universe waits to be discovered.

Let us perforate oblivion. Because oblivion is the thick rind around our origins.

The initial sin is a sin of memory. We will never get to the end of time.

I will end up with nothing saved out of this attempt to pull free of the yoke of words, attempt which, one day, got stuck in its own swamp.

The book belongs to the book.

Elya, it was written that we would rejoin you where we had thought we were leading you.

There is no help against this night.

APPROACHING THE GROUND OF THE BOOK

The word is a bud that stays closed, a flower of late seasons.

1

It seemed obvious to you that after the day you would think of conjuring up the night, that after having used words you would think of silence.

But you could not interfere with the unfolding of your work. Each of its pages had to use its guaranteed right to its own death.

And so the book would disappear in the book.

Oh Yaël, your name, broken at the far end of silence, was restored in death. But who was it took such poor care of it?

Its letters got scrambled by accident, and an unfamiliar name, "ELYA," formed on the sand where it had been a long time since anybody had expected anybody.

It is to my death that the book speaks, and I do not know my death.

My truth in the book is my truth outside life.
Thus my life grows around my books.

I write by the light of what is not revealed in what I express.

Suffering doubly from a silence without words and from words already again silent.

Named before you have been, death will take your name from you.

Life always comes *after* the book, as being comes *after* the face, *after* the landscape where we observe, meditate, or love.

First there is anxiousness, then something like pain . . .

To question, question in the hope of being healed by the answer.
But are questions not heady with a suffering to be deciphered, a means to break your suffering through that of others?

Between me and myself there are innumerable words whose ways and will I do not know. They move me away from the book which, sentence by sentence, has moved away from them.

This is how death lets us live its impossible dream of life.

I do not at all mind that a work I had lost sight of should find its continuation in the empty space which reaches all the way to the ground of the book I am now going to penetrate, less sure of myself than of the pages I am drawn to.

Silence, like the writer, knows the anguish of the word which will break it with cruel love.

Yaël survives in our dread of suffering. Could there be a road for us even in death?

Where shall I stop?—but perhaps I have only explored the large where the book engulfs the book.

We read ourselves in the ocean.

We are silent on the bare sand.

2

In the schoolyard, recess is in full swing. But who is this child who chooses to be off to the side, who is dreaming—looks as if he is dreaming—propped against the wall?

"His name is Elya," a boy of the same age tells his playmate.

"Ah," says the other. "Too bad for him."

They stared at him for a brief moment, then forgot.

On a milestone, his back to the road, Elya examines the snowy landscape above the camp where the young people with whom he has come to the mountains are milling about, singing, laughing.

"Come down, Elya," he heard them shouting. "Time for breakfast."

A girl came to get him.

"They are calling you, Elya," she said. "You've got to obey."

"They are calling me from all sides," he replied. "As I can't go everywhere, I'll stay."

She left in tears.

In the late-afternoon crowd a man, Elya, makes his way home to the outskirts of town.

He neither sees nor hears.

He seems chosen among all to simplify the ever-complex relations between absence and the disturbed world of silence.

"Elya . . . Elya . . . Elya . . ." I shouted.

The sky was an immense wad of cotton. I crawled through a hostile universe, not seeing any exit.

THE GROUND OF THE BOOK

The desert does not come to the end of ending.
The ocean puts an end to not ending.
Where is the end, you said, if not beyond death,
in the scattered remains of hope?

It was in Elya that you lost yourself, Yaël. In him
you fell silent.

O death, final page read without flagging, yet
never exhausted.

The book is for the exile what the universe is for
God.
So any book of exile is God's place.

All is dead, and you think you are living.
You are at the threshold. Left alone to fight.

The threshold remains to be defined.
A sunny day, perhaps?

Under the ashes there is homage to fire
which you can hear.

Man is All. God is Nothing. Here is the riddle.
To glide towards Nothing. Perennial slope.

A Puddle of Water

("The book," I was told by a sage I sincerely respect, "contains a face which we wrinkle in writing.

"The older the book the purer the face."

And he added: "Do not believe that the book [which is not spared illness] disappears with the book. It dies only in its filigree. We know it is up to us to look for it beyond where it will give us back our written world."

He said further: "A lake is at the peak of power because it is master over the reflections which haunt it. Likewise the book when it lets us hear and drink.")

Rain had left a puddle in the street, several inches deep, which the mud made into a lake buried in its misery.

However, the sun played there at inventing colors and getting them to correspond.

I was watching this unexpected concert of reflections when, suddenly, a car turned the corner, barreled across the puddle and splashed me.

Is the book, in its beginning, a puddle like this whose music enchanted me for a minute or, rather, the muck on my flannel pants like flakes of a wilted page where writing was tackled?

I was waiting for Yaël. —Why, in fact, was I waiting for her when she was dead?—Paris, moreover, had been basking in a radiant sun for a whole week.

This puddle is maybe Elya, a forbidden brew, Elya as you might imagine him, not knowing his life. But his life, threatened all the short while it lasted, had it not had the face of an eternal child bend over it so closely as to take on its features?

We have not done fighting when we die. The seasons bathe in rotting water as in the short-lived rainbow beginning to fade. They burn out in what was their reason to be.

When we met, Yaël, we had arrived, though still young, at the end of our wandering: you becoming a word, and I, parallel, a man of the Letter.

Nothing, however, let us know our time was so measured we could no longer retrace our steps.

Face to face, accomplices, hangmen, victims of a silence of dream and flesh which you had nourished in your soul and guts and which, little by little, had become our only resort, our only chance of liberation.

Cherished in his absence, this natural son of Nothing was going to take everything from us. He appropriated (without a fair fight) the book in the name of a truth which excluded us, you because of me, and me through you. A truth to which we would return with our regrets, our memories, and this need to survive which makes us insist insolently at the threshold.

Cursed in our consciousness of speaking and in our heedless pretention to succeed in it.

Our route is that of the great sinners for whom God is a dawn secret without ties and which bleeds.

2

. . . like a secret and more than a buried word. Our desire to love is as strong as the night's power over the sap in trees, and as possessive.

Our tree is a nocturnal plant which will never bear fruit. But sometimes stars fall asleep on its gigantic branches.

Hence an infinite silence in the quick of a wound which will never

scar over. Through this opening you have entered the book, Yaël.
Through a similar opening you expulsed Elya.

In death, the body is on the scale of the world.

> *(Ah, to think that a puddle can hold the sky*
> *which comes after the sky and defies the sun.*
> *Night has the last word.)*

You came towards me. I had seen you from a distance. How beautiful you were, Yaël. Death had not changed you.

> *(Our days are recorded on the yellowed page of*
> *the sky,*
> *at the last sight of the herb of renunciation.*
> *O time of the implacable fullness of times.)*

The Broken Mirror of Words

To be born in death, to be stillborn, O implosive immortality of God.

1

When he realized that the Word had a face and that Silence had one likewise, he understood that man, in what he introduces or keeps unsaid, has now the face of God, now that of His absence.

"God," she had said to me, "I carried him in my belly close to nine months. When those violent contractions and cramps of more than my flesh announced the hour of His birth everything around me died.

"God was dead with the birth of my child."

Of all the stories I was able to put together Elya's is certainly the most extraordinary.

Yaël refused to let me come near it. Interpretations and questions ran up against her resistance.

So the book took shape against the grain of the book.

(It will never be just another story like those in-

*crusted in your memory, but one more star in the
night.*

*I would exaggerate if I pretended to have dis-
covered it. One evening, it caught my eye with all
sorts of tricks, no doubt hoping to become finally
luminous in it. For it was a star from the ranks of
useless celestial bodies, but my eyes would perhaps
tell its erratic, passive life.*

*The sky had taken refuge in my eyelids, airy and
black like Yaël's shadow. In the middle, the boldest
knot of nothing defied with serene opposition the
fine screen of time.*

O void weaned on the first evening of the world.)

. . . so the book took shape against the grain of the word, in the
empty space where, because of the inexplicable resignation of the
stars, the dark wielded its dissolving power over the night.

It is in this void that writing is most risky. A stillborn child took it
on. We will make every word into an impregnable fortress with determined stones. Because where everything has been said death
concentrates on its defense against life's siege. Here, words enter
the eternity of the word whose roads are inward like Elya's which
we took one day without worrying too much about the lurking danger of being suffocated.

But where did we hope to go? We could only destroy ourselves in
order to reign absent over our ruins.

In the furrow of God.

2

I entered the word stealthily, and my embarrassment amused
you.

I took your place. But you, where were you?

For a time we became the same word. It could not last. There was
a moment when we could no longer fit our voices to our speech.

You talked to yourself
before any word.
You could not do anything for me
or for anybody else.

Divine solitude: a word outdistanced.

3

"And what comes about without the word, in the spoken word?"
"Perhaps you?"
"Perhaps me?"
"Perhaps the world?"

4

For the One, *the other* is a personified beyond.
You say "elsewhere," as one might beg "to finally
be."

*(I speak . . . but to whom? And why speak? For
whom? How? With what aim, in which light,
which perspective? To speak—under what pretext,
to which end? Ah, to go up to where and where
from? To stop at which frontier, in which dark or
flame, on which beach or mountain?*

*To speak—under what circumstances, after
what silence, wave, or incomparable path in mid-
ocean, after what question, desert, exile, before
which dawn?*

*I speak—in what summer, after what long win-
ter, what call, what failure, before what scream?*

—After what death, before what death?)

The stone, one evening, stopped seeing the stone.

Indifference of the void.

5

This desire to make what was into what is and, then, what is into what will last leads us to supplant the human face by another which we want inviolable the better to encircle it.
Seed grain is our saving plank.
One day it will turn over in the raging sea where it now floats.
And we will sink for having tried the impossible.

In what distress you were, Yaël, ruse of God, immortal sister of the Void.

6

(Truth is also the span of time a lie hesitates, is, let us say, distracted.
We build on this.

Black rose of the secret. Only silence could be born from the word in its glory.
God spoke once in order to seize His word.

What will my reflection make of me? Perhaps the man I once was.

Without body, You are without speech, but riddled with writing.
Writing: wrought crystal of silence.

Sometimes there is such conviction in lies that truth is confounded.

Hesitant Yaël, distracted Yaël, lucid Yaël, did
you know you bore truth all by yourself, in a body
with a single deadline?
        The way the universe bore God.)

7

Ah, to save what was the true instant of a truth
impossible to save.

God faces God, and the book the book.
Night is cut off from the night by a light which burns it. Words
stay forever separate.
And the writer? He is like the earth which turns on itself and
around a slower light whose near and far sides he explores.
Like the earth, he would love to be the center of the universe.
Frightening solitude of the world, of God, of man.
God leans on God, the book on the book, man on his shadow.
While a word awakens other words, silence raises no echo. Si-
lence only prolongs silence.
With you, Yaël, the word left the book. So what kind of a book is
this, wordless, each of its letters retracing an absent gesture? A book
denounced by the book, it can only be read in the broken mirror of
words.

(To withdraw, ah, to be engulfed behind the last
shadow, the last scream, the last silence of my
books,
        and go green.
        and go again green.)

8

. . . but the story is here present, absent in its limpid new starts.
There once was a book. There still was a book yesterday, and the
same book will be there tomorrow.
You never left me, Yaël. Alive or dead.
Desperately lost in a world which has not been since its first day.

Silence is the painful intuition of a word destined for *the other*.
Day breaks elsewhere.
Our actions are of the night.

Your step no longer hears your step.
Your hand is your guide.

(God is the reality of Nothing.)

9

Stillborn, you knew and forgot everything at the
same time.

If God is all childhood,
Elya could have been God.
If God is all innocence,
Elya could have been God.
If God is all knowledge,
Elya could have been God.
If God is all absence,
Elya could have been God.
For Elya was born of his death
and died of his birth.

For God was born of His absence
and died of knowledge.
O Yaël, word free of God,
in vain your voice where nothing moves.

*(And suddenly your speech, Yaël, began to twist,
to turn large, crazy circles in space where I could
not see you.*

Silence was torn in a thousand plaintive pages.

*Death whitewashes evil, O unmarriageable, un-
measurable page.)*

From Day to the Shadow of Day

1

The book is the place where a writer offers his voice up to silence.

Hence every margin is the beach of an avowal held back. And on its edge, the words gather and seal their alliance with the sea.

My bible is the page you cannot choose.

2

What can a stone reply to the charge that it is hard except that it is hard to last?

Tell me which road you take, and I will tell you who you will become, whom you will join.

1

All is created. You remember nothing. You see all.

One day, I learned my name from my books. You were not with me. I broke into the world which was going to be ours. The road stretched before me, split the horizon.

Nothing subsists in death, so memory is queen.

One day, I saw myself in all the stages I had gone through. My memories had gorged on memories down through the centuries.

So that I cannot tell in what era, on which continent I was born.

"The road taken by a Jew," some sage said, "is the imperceptible course of a drop of water from the mountain top to the sea."

I will have been a Jew in my course.

> *(No roll of parchment holds a sentence of mine copied by hand. I write on the flimsiest, least durable material which perfectly suits the words relieved of my death.)*

So I will have been a Jew in the legitimate lightness of my pen.

God, in the book, can stand only God.

This Judaism after God, my kind, is a lake over which my questions hover like mountaintops, some of them out of reach. The lake has given birth to the river on which I have traveled without paying too much attention to the landscape, subdued by the absolute in motion which would flood me with the day.

Even the most daring diver could not separate the words in my books from the sentences written in the vast bottom of the sea where any question dies of its questioning.

The same death indefinitely opts for the same man.

My work bears witness to this as if from the extreme point of my being, at the dawn of all end and all birth.

I will have been a Jew for not being able to answer to any but myself, more of a stranger than anyone else, and close to the poorest in the losing word.

*(. . . of a certain Judaism which takes its force
and features from the word and is contemporary
with the book.*

*Deprived of God in His equivocal death where
the creature's fate is a baroque pattern of writing.*

*"O my lover," cried Yaël, "who was ever closer to
the word than you who came to love it when it was
gently silent?")*

2

Jew, for you the homeless fruit of aggressive
silence.

So, with God dead, I found my Jewishness confirmed in the book,
at the predestined spot where it came upon its face, the saddest,
most unconsoled that man can have.

Because being Jewish means exiling yourself in the word and, at
the same time, weeping for your exile.

The return to the book is a return to forgotten sites.

God's heritage could only be handed on in the death He ushered
in.

At the end of our lives, with all tasks done, we will in turn hold up
the book of our apprenticeship.

*(Circular work; you must tackle my work in its
circles.*

And each of them will demand a new reading.)

3

The day's freedom consists in the light's secret
climb back to the beginnings of the shores deserted by men.

The heart beats in the emptiness of the astonished body. Its form will come from *the other*.
Thus the world will form the world in freeing it.
Thus God, within Himself, will come to terms with the Face.

The sage dipped his reed pen into the inkwell, pulled it out, and held it for a few moments, as if in doubt, above the page where he had not noted anything yet that day. Then, to his pupil's surprise, he drew a small circle in a corner of the blotter he always kept within reach.

"This circle," he said, "which the blotter has made into a point invaded by night, is God."

"Why did you want the circle to turn into a black point? And why should this stain among so many others on your blotter be God?" the disciple asked.

"Your question is that of the Lord," replied the sage.

"If my question is that of the Lord," said the disciple, "I know now that God has created me in His image."

4

At this time before time, when life was only a sickly death with weak lungs, one small point in space contained, like a bubble, all the wanderings of the worlds.

When it burst it freed the universe, but gave form to exile.

God had disappeared, existing only in Creation.

Being the Principle of Unity—a circle tightening in the infallible memory of the circle—He was going to become the dazzling center of clear absence.

Never again will we escape exile.

The book is among its true stages.

*(In death there are myriads of islands far be-
yond life—stars, stars which life devours.*

*A word without destiny, an unpronounceable
name was the floral ornament of our page.*

We shall stomp on our crowns.
We shall renounce our kingdoms.)

Counter-Test

With its stars of ink the book is a universe in motion which our eyes fix.

People of the Book, we will never have a house. We shall die in words.

Interpretation is bound to act on the fate of individuals and of the world. It gives their destiny a new course, taking full responsibility for it, being ready to suffer the consequences and pay the price.

Also, interpreting the Book means first of all rising up against God to take voice and pen out of His power. We have to get rid of the divine within us in order to give God back to Himself and fully enjoy our freedom as men.

Simplicity is the wisdom of summits.

From the outset it has been my own story unrolling before my eyes.

It cannot be yours because of course our routes differ, even though we share night as the womb from which we were one morning ejected.

All coincidence is leaven for existence against its dark finality. We moved the same milestones, but never knew where we were.

Riveted to space, to the place reserved for dreamers, we rest, delicate starfish, on the very bottom of the soul.

To accept life means proposing an explanation of existence. But which one could we adopt? They are all contradictory.

Purity of being at the two poles of innocence.

We intuit life only in its flight. Tomorrow will be another moment of the source.

Alliance of slack time and time woven. We shall never read the pages rejected from the book.

The space of a spark prolonged. Mock amazement.
You will not find God where He expects you, but where you expect the dawn.

You make awkward steps towards God—you run towards Nothing.

Divided, I will be innocently human, as opposed to God, wise and indivisible.

Not-knowing has knowing as its esplanade where God disclaims competence.

My hands are full when you give me your hand.
A feather of spray will never fly out of the well.

Night outside. Inside, lack of air, the flame consumed.
What darkness always weighs on the unsubdued paths of the soul.
Truth has no place. It is a glimmer of unlivable places.

You only sleep with one hand. The other spangles your sleep.
Skylights, skylights . . .

I aim to be, someday, seen.

What remains to be thought (the fruit) follows what has been thought (the tree). But there is something else unthought which is the irreducible desert where our steps are weighed down with the day.

Entering into God's thought means thinking the unthought.

Could divine presence, as glimpsed by the mind, be thought at the heart of the unthought infinite?—But all thinking rids us of God.

One writes before or after God.
God is the blank present.

Memory of a Dead Memory

Death left you your chance: a deadly season
without fruit.

The sea assimilates us to the wave. Up to us to
surge and wear down the rock.

After death, the sea takes our measure.

Time searched through the past and made inseparable faces
march by for us, ours among them. But Elya's was lacking.

You could not suppress a gesture of irritation, Yaël, and you said
to me:

"My memories will supplement those of the days. I have never
lived within time."

("... possibly dead"
—is how you described life close to our steps.)

After *Yaël, Elya.* After the word in ambush for the book, a book of
the refused word.

And as if autumn was only the falling of summer, and spring but
the fable of winter run down.

Nothingness is our All. The sky is a repeat of its own absence on
which the void bestows a relief of disintegrated constellations.

So that there is nothing at the beginning, nothing at the end but a
procedure caught in its hesitations and turns.

The beginning of the book is a beginning for being and things.

All writing invites to an anterior reading of the world which the word urges and which we pursue to the limits of faded memory.

We can only write what we have been able to read. It is an infinitesimal part of the universe to be told.

The book never actually surrenders.

> (*"I imagine a writer who cannot reread himself."*
> *"Imagine. Imagine."*
> *"I imagine a book which cannot be abridged."*
> *"Imagine. Imagine."*
> *"I imagine a word become night, become all nights."*
> *"To this word we were prey.")*

Speaking of the book, Yaël said:

"The word would have to revive before we could approach its life tied to ours with every syllable.

"But on what page, in what plausible space conquered outside time?"

And she added:

"What we take for a written page is only a wager, on the level of the letter, to appropriate man and the world—which could only be done on the morning of death."

On the threshold of a rejected birth we write in the shadow of what has been written, but never read.

The book veils itself in the book.

As God does in God.

The Book within the Book

The ground of the book rises like a terrace into the future. There takes place the fore-gesture, as it were, with which, after every stair innocently climbed, the writer embraces absence in the age of the book.

We believed the news of the book's premature disappearance: every page comments on it with its cuts, like a man who at any moment of his life tells a fragment of the story of his death so that it can be pondered.

Grebe, bird of sleeping waters,
The dark too knows how to fly.

Shall I reveal the book within the book by its stifled echoes: a secluded existence on the margin of ours, a senseless story of God?

At the time when your son was dying daily in your womb, Yaël, this book already lived his death within the book I was writing then and which borrowed your name. Is it not natural for this one now to have your child's name?

"Yaël must die through Elya. The four letters they share will join face to face and obliterate their origin. They will keep death on the alert. The book anticipates a time of alarm," I said to myself.

We will have crossed enemy lines together, the sparkling barbed wire of the void. You thought you were entering my room, but the door opened onto the night and its hooked lights.

I was thinking about the uncertain combat of man with his truth when you surprised me. And it seemed to me that your hands hid the incomparable book which all other books deny furiously in order to survive it.

But how can we deny ourselves where we must win? Or will it all happen as if, drunk with presence, we must at all costs tear from the All the exacting Nothing we represent?

You seemed to want to confide in me in your thirst for eternity. What a nightmare, Yaël. Had I not forced your heart to give in? Had I not died after you? You do not say a word. Our bodies meshed in an aftermath of effort. We were one and the same dark silence within the indissoluble silence of the world.

It seems indispensable to make these pages subservient to the secret, steady unfolding of this silence to which we will have to return often. Pages which I publish without changes. But this display will not make the dark withdraw. Protected silence where the word is in agony, but charitable words come for a time to help before they are set into the surface.

Yaël was not a finished book. *Elya* completes it in the original completeness where man and the world awaken.

> (*The void is fascinated by the elsewhere and enters, marveling, the void.*
>
> *Night dreams of more beautiful nights and is transfigured from star to star.*
>
> *The beyond multiplies us.*
>
> *God is the last* other.)

Pledge of the Abyss

1

(God gives death the dimensions of His absence.)

2

(To write as if addressing God. But what to expect from nothingness where any word is disarmed?

There is no far-off death.

Anchored in the night like one single diamond.

"What is memory?"
"A marvelous flight where all is black,
"a beautiful, luminous bird, soon to be black too."

Being means questioning. Means interrogating yourself in the labyrinths of the Question put to others and to God, and which does not expect any answer.

Night of mystery, total night.
Dawn will be a shock.

Night is the last to speak to absence.

Only what disappears will have called for us.

What did you hope for, what, if not to die the death of the lips in the word voted in.

If ever you should judge my book pernicious you could, according to rabbinical recommendation, burn one half and bury the other.
But it will nonetheless stay written in space, as if each of its syllables were lit up by day or kindled by the dark in order to die of the dawn and rebound from a star.

All I know has come to me from reading the book, from its omens of nakedness, its nightly legibility.

The man who questions takes part in a universal interrogation with an abyss at its center. The book's configuration allows for this: it is the last circle of softened words.

No doubt your God needed a name in upper case to be struck honorably high.

Name too large for my mouth, will I never pronounce you? You are spared by your illicit absence.

"If You are able to punish, O Lord," said an insane mystic, "You should be able to punish Yourself.
"At the sight of evil whose very idea I cannot bear, do no longer veil Your face, but bruise Yourself without mercy.
"I shall be washed in Your guilty blood."

*Vulnerable through whatever lays me open or
smothers me, like the night, like the morning.*

*When it is time to leave the book I go back to it,
as if from the pit of my resolution there emerged an
irresistible command of the besieged page to recon-
sider it.*

*Thus we go into the death our feet had unwit-
tingly trod on.*

*Through such repeated renewals, in night's slow
rhythm, the light reaches the day.*

*Hope is bound to writing. And what greater
hope than that of the feverish, hungry man for
whom reading and adventures are selective seeds?*

*In my search for origins I have never really
known which roads I took. They are so varied, so
many.*

Any beginning ends when it is marked.

*The exordium finds its conclusion in tomorrow's
stubborn silence.*

We were walking along the Seine, Yaël. I remember it well. Near
the Pont-Neuf, some weeks before my crime.

You suddenly said to me: "My stillborn child was in the image of
the world. God's life is a life surrounded by emptiness. We daily
watch how the forbidden flora of universal death, which precedes
our own, blossoms on our banks."

The glory of the book is posthumous.

Birth of Self

1

(The other has a head start of more than one night. To catch up with him we would have to jump over the abyss.

A work round like the world where All moves towards All and Nothing towards Nothing in its legitimate will to be.

We will die a bartered death at the feet of our words.)

The adolescence of writing is that moment when something is on the verge of being said.

Some words die as children.

Word pledged to an unretouched death. Life is too narrow for the book to pass through.

I was born from a laborious reading of the night which my work has ever since suggested to you.

But as no work can be defined except in relation to other work, my life in the book is offered as an introduction to all lives fulfilled in the word.

Through the reinstated sign I rejoin man in his priority.

Where you are I am but the evening of our paired shadows.

The hours agree to the insane demands of the light. You are crazy in dreams, wise on the day of retreat.

Give up your place to the word. Richness does not come from us.

Accept what you cannot give. You will have the impression of giving everything else.

The book draws your image. Do people know that it obliterates you?

Where you pass the word has passed by.

Our days were militant. What exists was won by force. We have not neglected anything.

Three candles repeat the book because we made three century-old demands which continue to melt at the ends.

In God I dance.

"A flame," you said, "is, to the mind's eye, a mad rebirth of the world."

For us, Yaël, everything started from there. And the book takes its ashes into account.

But the formula how to go on living when you are thus evicted from yourself—who will tell us?

We take turns squandering our fortunes. Night will never learn to see.

Yaël said:
"When I call to God, I call to the Sense of the Void. O my love, my lover, you who go away, you do not know yet what it means to be alone. You do not know what it means to have your eyes fixed on the abyss.

"Our shrouds are woven of all our solitude. We will rest in the linen of our like lives.

". . . but what is it all about if not knowing what no one knows and what everyone looks for within himself as if the secret beat within our bodies, in each warm point of our blood.

"Knowing if the dawn is our field of light.

"Knowing if noon is our careers' crest.

"Knowing if the dusk is our last glance.

"The night hesitates before the forbidden night. This moment's hesitation clinches the vertigo above the abyss, salutary halt at the fatal edge of time.

"Even death is afraid of death."

God is more afraid of God than man.

It is to be asked if God is not the one inadmissible question, the deep avowal of this inadmissibility through which the world is cut off from the world and man from his divine ancestry.

On the earth you must walk; in the earth, imprison your steps where your frail questions hoist themselves like spikes of flowers.

God speaks where the word folds.
The word fertilizes the soil, not the sky.

Be wakeful so that your return to the native country will be accompanied by bees, true to the signal.

2

I am not born for others, nor for myself.
I am born, that is all.

The dark of my certainty
is a night of solitude.
Blind.

Lost.
Can you hear me?
I talk. I talk. I talk.
All this happened
before your death
and mine
when we housed the same desire
and followed the same road.
It happened yesterday
in the fog,
once upon a time in blood.
Barred doors,
in vain we will knock
on your gross panels.
There is no time
of rest.

The center is the moment. If God is the center He cannot exist except momentarily.

Therefore God passes in whatever, by virtue of renewing itself, does not pass.

Eternity is constant renewal. So that entering eternity means becoming conscious of all that begins all the time, means becoming yourself a beginning.

We find God at the outset of the book. God again tied to God.

The world changes within the world. *The Other* opposes *the Same* which it continues with its face.

> (. . . *this* other, *Yaël, this otherworldly being
> who was our painful obsession, who by not being
> attracted us like the void, and whom time could not
> destroy because he was the indifferent becoming of
> time. This same other, this same otherworldly
> being at the edge of our death, at the end of the
> forest in flames: what name could we choose for*

him, what face suggest? God is always in search of God.)

Face with many faces, we understand that God could confuse it with His own in the mutinous moments of a metamorphosis which excluded Him.

God dies with us wherever He shows Himself.

Man asserts and effaces himself by looking. Lies are bound to truth like the corolla to the seed. The self-image they show causes the most varied interpretations which evidence confirms.

Lies prompt us, suggesting means of self-realization. They place us in the only valid position, that of challenging ourselves.

In writing, truth is perhaps the scream. Sentences dress it up.

God and the universe are only an infinite glance destroyed.

(Faced with lies, death and truth nevertheless protest against being thought simple negation of the world. Both want to be sources of permanence. They hold the key to space.

Refractory margins, moving, dismantled, the rock will forever be beaten by the tide.

Virile word—the silence it let loose wears it away.

We write in its wound, at the first lull of the waves.)

In Bright Sunlight, the Gesture

*(Here I have to stress how strongly the word is
attracted to the nothing around it for which it is
the preferred prey.*

*It is the same attraction God has for the universe
of the ultimate utterance.*

*There was once, before evening, a more intimate
evening when God spoke.*

*Yaël, word for word you have recaptured His
speech.*

*Page by page, we answer the end of the world
with our own end.*

Stars and creatures dart their twin rays.)

A gesture. And you realize it was an essential gesture. But the
moment you made it you did not think of this. Death spoke within
you. Death became the strength of your fists, your fingers, their bitter resolution.

You wanted to live. You acted. You saved yourself by giving death.
But in fact you made it a longer death. You were dead before, in
Yaël, dead at your birth. You had to go back to your point of depar-
ture. Death, we know, is the return to the egg.

The promptness of your gesture excluded premeditation. Its apparent inconsistency (had you not, after all, accepted your compan-
ion's behavior?) could at first sight have passed it off as a gratuitous

gesture. But is gratuitousness not a needle giddy with its point, salt-covered peaks at the confines of margins and silence?

Girl, girl, gratuitousness has the gravity of a girl on the crumbly summits of time.

No one alive has access to the margins. Their silence is a world ruled by night.

You had to overcome, at Yaël's side, the hostility of borders. Death surrenders only to death.

You became the toy of a sordid machination for which Yaël was responsible as much as you. Beloved Yaël, Yaël stroked in her most voluptuous nakedness so that you could use your power as lovers and, through the lazy passion of your entangled bodies, enter the void in the name of the ruling truth.

In bright sunlight, in the bright human day.

The Transparency of Time

Light through a crystal turns me inward, anxious to reflect rather than inflect my image.

Trying to unravel an enigma I have turned in vain all around my reflection.

Which of us two is real?

—as he is not I, I am no longer he, but another who surreptitiously stole my features in his desire to remain *the other*.

This time—like a book. All these books will have allowed us to do our time.

A certainty. And it will have granted us nothing.

1

What is writing or birth if not a signal to the word or creature that they are due?

The end will be our time. But death is in the simplest, in the soft heart of the rind.

In other eyes, being means becoming, whereas in ours it means, one day, having been.

I am in whatever bears my name and continues when I am interrupted. The world does not exist except in mysterious references to a past world. I do not exist except in relation to the space of a word uttered.

Between the word heard and the word to be said, in this half-
silence which is the last refuge of the echo, there is my place.

Day is pale at its birth. Thus man trembles at the most fragile
point of love.

All clarity has come to us from the desert. My work is a book of
sand, not only in its light, but in its stark nakedness.

A word is tiny in its scope of revelation, immense in the scanti-
ness of the sign. The book is always open.

Every day helps us lose the last.
God remains our largest erasure.

2

The world organizes itself in terms of its pre-
meditated end.

You can love only what you can destroy or what
daily destroys you.
Such is the love of God.

What to expect of death except what it takes
from us: ourselves?

Tomorrow has the respectability of an elaborate
absence.

Time carries off time. The word gets a tan on the
mountains.
Black are the words of the book.

Survival is perhaps the obsessive memory of a

spoor which we are alone to witness within the spoor.

The line will be of light.

The star was a message of health. We realize that death, in the course and at the end of the road, is only an exhausted word dramatically giving in to the voracious dark.

Sun, stemless yellow dahlia, where there is no Paradise.

I was born with the sun," said Yaël. "I was born of a haphazard voice while the eye listened.

"Dawn puts the earth to the Question. We talked as long as it was light. One word was set against another. We disappeared with the dusk.

"What was approved will be squandered, vault turning pale with gems, O stammering in the letter.

"Our oath was homage to the silence in which you tore out the leaves of the book."

3

Dawn is the blessed coming of the bond, the pact with the prow pressing to be applied.

Only the passage is planned, only the ocean launched.

Reality is in the folding of a wounded wing.

Complacently other, but like the star riveted to the void, our time blurs with us in time, its arms full of years.

Who are you, O who are you if not the woman
who answers to my urgent, stabbing need to be
recognized in my delirium by loved eyes?

Death widens the impasse.

Eye of grain, eye of granite.

We sprout and grow stiff with the same giddiness.

The adventure of looking (mutual need to see and be seen) leads
man into a confounding examination of himself and the world, each
depending on the other, each annulled through the other in con-
fessed impotence and hunger which writing on the bottom of the
abyss takes on with its last bit of strength.

In its extremities, light is opaque. We explore wild ground in
back of the world.

At dawn, the sky was the tabooed face of a tortured man.

When man is threatened by time's arrow his
shield is not the word, but silence, the smooth,
solid, swelling silence the world glides on and
which you have made a weapon to fit your arm.

Stars, myriads of pierced eyes.
A blind universe sees God.

Silence is one step ahead of death.

It is in the middle of life that you learn to die, as
if till then death were but a deferred encounter.

Night is at the center of my wait.

Death—an empty dream?
To wander, wander as one breathes or talks.
Yesterday, tomorrow—two terms which, coupled, designate eternity.
Could the sun be inside us? Then morning would be the reassuring reflection of our soul.

Yaël, when you opened your eyes, did you know you were, paradoxically, at the beginning and end of your journey?

I think of those whose name is in the name of an almond, a wave, an avenue, and who will never be fruit, surge, branch.
I think of those who, between two distant shores of life, were the stubborn moment of a mast in foam and wind.
I think of those who, one evening, were crushed on the cliffs of a last look and whose bodies will forever float on the ocean of centuries.
Through their mediation God has entered our retina.

(My books testify to the impossible approach of His Name.

I have lived at an immense distance from the Kingdom I often thought I had reached.

If He did not exist I would have howled to His glory. I despise those who see Him, because they only look on themselves.

He is the invisible seer of an invisible world. O to make ourselves seeing to become His equals in nothingness.

You did not die, Lord, of having been, but of having thought You were.

Words have thought as their precipice.

The book tempts the universe and man with being read in their shared death.
Legitimate chance to endure.

Turning to the book must mean having guessed that we metamorphose in the word, that in it we promptly die.

Man of writing, you have the unlimited for your fence.)

For a man suffocating in the hold of a ship the point of convergence is the regulation porthole, before it turns into a beach unrelated to those on the globe.

We have trudged through its sand, our faces furrowed by the spindrift and salt of a periodical voyage.

Tomorrow also belongs to man.

Time is double in a word come from elsewhere.

(Where nothing was.
You are. You were.)

4

The word is in love with the perfect face as a seed is with its fruit: secretly and for the intuitive rise of the sap.

God is the accepted challenge of the word. But
the word does not lead to God. Only silence could.

This man is serious, and what he forbears to con-
fess is serious. His muteness has known the vicissi-
tudes of wrecks.

Seed-diamonds, stars powdered for a star.

The earth's core could only be hypothetical seed, not of diamonds, but of nickel and iron. Death's complex growth, layer by
layer, of which the earth is an example.
The circle is contained in the stone and grows in circles.

So terror and fear of death were nothing but terror and fear of
truth.
A lie would then seem to be an impersonal reply to the onslaught
of heaven, a providential trump of our lust for life. But the face persists, witness of our destructions.
Ah, to destroy ourselves in flowers, in leaves, in flames.

Form makes us.

Gravity is the exhausted sister of the freedom which eludes our
will and incites us, once sobered, to ask the question of the first
vigil, namely, how far have we left ourselves behind in promises, in
exile, in death?

What we call death is but death transformed into another death
bearing our name—an end concerning only us within what has no
end.

Thought is tied to the flesh. A dead thought is a body sacrificed.

Led to believe death imperishable, we perish from a failure of
memory.

Hence eternity is without image, without voice.

A couple making love is a shadow crossing the night.

Memory of what is without memories. The void attests the vastness of the thought which tries to find itself in nothingness.

O Yaël, your eternity builds up in the blank pages that made us fertile.

There is an after-death which is death appeased.

5

"You were listening to the book."

". . . not the book, but some of the lines written in it."

"You were listening to some of the lines written in the book."

". . . not lines written in the book, but my voice gone dead."

"You were listening to your voice gone dead."

". . . not gone dead, but suddenly far off, without echo, its timbre a blank."

"You were listening to day break."

". . . not day break, but the banishment of a strange light, taunted by the sun of adversity."

"You were listening to the moan of a strange, belittled light reverberating in space."

". . . not an autonomous light, but the reverberating moan of a light, sacrificed, the captive shadow of a sovereign radiance inseparable from eternity."

"You were listening to the night."

". . . not the night, but the receptive emptiness around a star, some clear sentences fallen from the star without sound."

"You were listening to a large fragment—perhaps all—of the ground of the book."

". . . not all of it nor a large fragment, but some of its outskirts."

"You were listening to a moment of the road taken, lost again with the road."

". . . not a moment lost or taken of my road, but its uprooted trees, its fruit scattered on the defiled threshold of the book."

THE BOOK

O Yaël, you lived dying of your gradual life.

Great is the freedom of light at the hour the sky grows dim.

You accepted the future we had forged for you, Elya, as we, in spite of ourselves, accept a past which was ours only in the book dictated to us.

Dead, alive—this could not be important.

The past, the future from now on form one same grey sky, one enormous opening beset by clouds.

Door I
(The Margin)

This long toiling underground, on both sides of death, ah some day this will be our royal way.

"What are you waiting for? What are you waiting for? Death, of course. But what else?"
"The return to death."

Slice of claimed eternity. Time watches the days disperse in order, along with men.
Our obedience deserves a reward.

Swan—bird of margins.

In the half-light of the room (it was still night outside), the threefold mirror cracked in the middle—you will remember that Yaël unfortunately broke it when she was about to give birth and, alone in the bedroom, had taken some object to throw against the door in the hope that her landlady would hear—in the room's half-light, the threefold mirror showed off its wound which in the faint rays announcing morning looked like a bloody vagina. Narrow crack of life and death which a woman in love offers him who takes her, I have seen a child come out between its lips paired for the best and the worst. I have seen the child become an adolescent under my eyes, the adolescent find himself a man, me, with my face, but without name.

What was I doing in this house, in this room? My steps had led my steps. Could God have been begotten, like us, by a mirror?

My steps had led my steps to you, Yaël, locked in, half-naked, inside a word I did not dare cross. I settled inside too. There you were, telling our story. There was Elya, asleep, and I listening. You said, we had died with your son. You said that your son now lived in our death.

In the womb where our beginnings conspire, did the condemned child once appeal to his eyes to take in the infinite? A miserable and magnificent look through the thick maternal flesh closed in its roundness.

That day, Yaël must have felt him move in her womb. Then the child drowned in the water of inhospitable seas.

Will I let this story drain like a net of dirty water? This story which, in its innocence, could have been that of Yaël's son and which he perhaps adjusted to in dying?

Life deprived of life in his mother-of-pearl body polished by the sand.

And could this tale with its unexpected curves and turns be the insatiable questioning of this presence from beyond oceans, loop tied in the loneliness of truth?

Inanimate and yet living with the life of an inspired thing. Called and obeyed.

The ocean sings in this child-shell where the heart has given way.

> *(How many of us dead left to save our image?*
> *We were told: "You have come. You are here."*
> *We scattered without seeing one another.)*

"Who am I?" Repetition is an achievement in its help.
"Who am I?" I answered.
Vegetal life struck by amaurosis.
O blindness, corolla of evil.

To every inch of garden its rose.
To every step a door pushed open.

Repetition is an achievement in its contingency.

>   *(Who knows but what the bottom of the abyss is
>   the mournful space of a descending scale whose
>   last note suddenly turned to stone.)*

Memory is perhaps the most faltering of all traces.

>   *(This unproved descent with the risk, for who
>   undertakes it, of perishing of a gesture as provok-
>   ing as the blind man's who carves a path through
>   the light—this descent, is it not an experience of
>   the far slope of desire which has, once and for all,
>   vowed the brushwood to the fire?
>   We are thwarted at the heart of our limitations.)*

Repetition is an achievement in its order.

You thought you could enter the book by the front door.
Did you not know, Yaël, that the face is in dispute there?
You could not be received in your own name.
Foolhardy insect in the spider web.
   —Did you not notice how much the moment rounds itself at the
first sign of a sentence?
   We were, in turn, the fibre and filigree of the page, the spreading
peacock's tail of writing and the everlasting menace of death.

We die, in a ring, of our rumors.

"Who am I?" Repetition is an achievement in its transcendence.
"Who am I?" I replied.

He would be called "Aely." He would be called "Elya." No matter. She was Yaël, recruit and rival of God.
Truth had chosen her belly to dwell in. A truth with a forehead, eyes, genitals, a soul.

> *("And he will be my plain.*
> *And I will be his terrace.*
> *And he will be my valley.*
> *And I will be his hill.*
> *And I will look at him.*
> *And he will look at me.")*

Light within light, inexhaustible, lighting up only itself.
At no moment does morning get lost.

> *("Yaël, have you not loved?"*
> *"Perhaps," she answered, "perhaps I have, but with a suppressed love which has never seen the day.")*

Although I was born on April 16 in Cairo, my father inadvertently declared to the consul's office making out my birth certificate that I was born on the 14th of that month.
Is it to this error in calculation I unconsciously owe the feeling that I have always been separated from my life by forty-eight hours? The two days added to mine could only be lived in death.
As with the book, as with God in the world, the first manifestation of my existence was an absence which bore my name.

*(You affirm what is. But what is, is not. In that
case, the real task of knowledge would be to deny
what is in order to grasp what is not.*

"O lesson of death."

*"What is not: that is to say, what has been chal-
lenged in its appearance and what acknowledges
change and, in changing, is no more what it was
than what it will be.")*

Repetition is an achievement in its deliverance.
"Who am I?" I replied.
The void postpones any encounter with the void.
The sun has no double.

Yaël's child was already one hundred eighty days of blooming
death old. Modeled in thought and in flesh. Six months which life
could not imprint, but claimed nonetheless. Six months, like a slice
of eternity become eternity itself for lack of having been sized up.
Six months stranded weightless on an unknown island.

("Yaël, have you loved?"

*"Perhaps," she answered, "but with a love spent
with the day.")*

A child of death will be Yaël's world. There, a caress is rash tenderness and embracing means hugging the wind.

The walls here profit from a particular attention of the hour. Soft
brush stroke bathed in white oil with a warmer sheen than secrets
told at noon. Every window has the top leaves as companions and in
winter some bare branches.

We put our elbows on the window sill and counted the seasons.
We did not budge from our places.

We saw time dissolve.

"Who am I?" I asked.
"Who am I?" I replied.
Repetition is an achievement in its difference.

The absurd gesture denounced, rejected. But planned action urges us to circumvent the essential moment it governs.
For the one who dictates, however, as for the one who bows, the knife is the current and cutting resort.
Prince or slave—our lives are priced.
Man come back to his senses will adapt.

> *(Thus the seasons expose themselves and expi-*
> *ate, from the absorbent skin of roots to the frame,*
> *from sunken soil to the hollow skull of the sky.)*

Density of a crowd caught in its impatience to love, to create, to proceed to its certain goal. Heavy cluster faced with the lightness of God. Awakening of consciousness matured by reefs. The ocean grumbles with revolt against the port.
Candor of the sign. Tomorrow, who will read between the lines of the book the disheartening defeat of our supernatural conquest of the universe with its echo of man's dissatisfaction, man whom the waves wash ashore with fringes of black foam?

Tomorrow, who will read your distorted name on the forehead of a star, Yaël? Face whose disappearing is like a flake chipped off a chandelier, a tear whose reflections are clouded by the premature freezing of the spring?

Life and death: waiting subject to waiting.
Rigor of the act with the stiff nobility of a beacon where the light is swept by a dark swollen with light. Always turning, knowing its duty, and never as free. Dawn will warm its stones.

Hit by a bullet in full flight, a bird is nailed to his fall down to the ground.
A bloodstain marks the new place of the border stone. Everything ends with the trace where man does not end.

Your son, Yaël, is this ravaged dream awakened by the great white owl, winged phantom of the night expanse, which ambushes its prey from the top of the oldest dike of the years.
We breathe on ruins.

(White owl, are you the spoken word when you feverishly row through the air? Owl, are you the written word when you land on a docile twig?
Are you the same bird each time?
The world claims hand and mouth. But your son, Yaël, what lamp of welcome morning will remind you of his body so that you could restore it according to your heart and iris?)

Canvas of days without generating force which will not be mentioned anywhere. Death places its margins. You assemble. You sew.
The embroidery speaks to the needle of a different life, of a whole unsuspected, other flora. Planted, fire has sprouted, has bloomed. In the mud of night, seeds gleam. But does not the corolla at the top miraculously bear witness to the burst of roots we take so long to get a glimpse of?
The wound has the rose as childhood friend.
The elsewhere is still our earth.

Where do you turn, Yaël, when you want to find yourself and be a mother in your child's happiness? From one end to the other of a preponderant passion.

Light is revived joy. Like a flame under a glass globe which eventually lacks air.

.

The world is in your lap.

The elsewhere is still our strength, our theme, our law.
Ecumenical, while we possess our corner where we stretch out
side by side.

Yesterday Elya would have been ten years old. Tanned, with blue
eyes. In his grey vest, his suede tie bought in Spain, his long pants.
And this irresistible smile. A young man stood before us. Yaël gave
him his present: a wristwatch in its case.
He blushed and came up to kiss her.
"One moment," he said. And disappeared.
Yesterday is the past of the night which governs us.
We have only our shadows to move with at night.

(Night cracks wherever the sun appears.
Our walls are replaced with thicker walls.)

How far will you push painting the portrait of the child whom the
void has taken from you and over whom you have no hold?
You are getting weak. Soon you will break down.
Night is judge.

A dreaming child, dreamed in the meandering of a rebellious
mind. Tragically alone. In the conditioned space in the back of the
mind, vast thicket where the world totters.
Ten years have passed. Soon it will be fifteen. He will have the
face of your lover, Yaël, and later mine.

He is the face.

(Hawkweed, perfidious plant which strengthens
the sight of the rapacious bird.
The hawk was your accomplice above the streams
of blood.)

At any rate, if he was in his unborn state the image of Yaël's de-
sire, he never gave up being himself. That is to say, being *the other*.
Thus he was close to us, both representing us and turning us out.
Thus he will have been both our defense and offense.

In the worst surrender of the loved woman, will I beg him to
come to my aid and, afterwards, blame him for not being me, or for
being so on his own account, as if by intuition or chance, as you
might turn a corner in the street and knock into a passer-by who
is—O mockery—your double?

Will I have helped, studied, admired him sufficiently within me
and then, sick of absence, in one swoop steal his voice and eyes in
order to substitute myself for this *other* whom he managed to ape?

O death, unthinkable exit where everything suddenly becomes
thinkable.

You are asleep, Yaël. Your womb was a night full of sleep.
Like sleepwalkers we will have run through time.

We will have run through the face and the fantastic world of the
face.

> *(You will never be able to encompass all my*
> *work. But if, one day, you should succeed you*
> *would see that a stillborn child was its bait and its*
> *silence.)*

You will never be able to encompass our alliances. Evil is in tow to
evil. The word remains the next threshold.

Thus it is elsewhere that everything started: in the depth of a
womb where misfortune came down and dislodged a disinherited
being whose form life did not dare question.

Thus it is against life that we have enshrined a man-child unburdened of his soul, violated in oblivion. Against the world we have received him: you, his mother and lover, and I, his lost chance.

(So many words, Elya, have swallowed the bait.
I have sacrificed you forever to my name.)

Door II
(The Name)

With your screams you have composed his name. And every scream is one of the letters which names you.

To learn my name from the letter. To spell and fear, to cherish and flee it.
To learn reading my life in the Book of the Dead.
Anguish glows above the ashes.
On the log the flame takes its revenge against the forest.
To reach the sky where the fire spreads.
Day recovers its unity.
Morning by
morning,
night by
night.

1

No reading of God is conceivable except in God.
Here, a wretched being will be read in his hunted life, beyond noise, beyond milestones.
No use to lock the door.
The book is in the lock.

"My God, the diapers. I have forgotten the diapers," said Yaël.

"Alas, your child does not need any."

"I have to have diapers for my angel," Yaël insisted.

"Your child hovers in your arms of air. As two thousand years of exile tenderly cradle the minute which does not recognize them."

The tree is taller than time.

God let go of God in death
and set himself up as an example.

(Continuity can only be assumed in the break by him who refuses to support its sterile excesses.
The chance of a road is as much in its memorable line as in its indeterminable openings.

The day that gives me flowers is my only favorite.)

Elya will go to school tomorrow. Elya started school yesterday. Elya can count up to ten. Elya will soon be able to count up to one hundred. He expresses himself like a grown-up. He is funny, curious. And strong. And brave. Independent and affectionate. Hanging on his mother's neck or trotting along beside her. His hair curls. Elya on a bicycle. He becomes more refined. He controls himself. His mother says: "He comes up to my shoulder now." Elya pays attention to what passes, to what becomes encrusted. The world attracts, the void fascinates him. He shows great maturity. Argumentative. Full of ideas and projects. He has eyes only for his mother. She sees nothing but him. How he has grown! She nevertheless feels younger since. He has left the university. With diploma, congratulations, and flattery. Everything seems easy for him. She watches him developing. What pride! She does not always understand him. She makes efforts not to disappoint him. She listens. She sometimes makes a note of his comments. He has become a man, her man. He is her constant preoccupation and her goal. He leaves, comes back, leaves again. How she ages when he is not there. Where is he? He has mentioned a girlfriend. How she suffers! Where is he? She snuggles against his chest, nestles in his arms. You might think they were lovers. He is her green truth, her tall tree full of fruit of a new taste. And handsome. He is her support, her nourishment. He is all her presence, her strength. He is her guardian. But where is he? Ah, here he comes. But what is the matter? Is this him? Her tree reeling, sick, Elya on the ground, no, not on the ground . . . but yes, exactly. Some cloud over him. Fog. A storm, maybe? He cannot resist. He cannot get up. Much fog, wind. Snow perhaps? How cold it is. What a night, O what a night. So many hours crumbled in their hope. Was the fallen tree hollow inside? The world had lain down on the world, but you, Yaël, you stayed upright, rising against the truth which ravished your soul. You joined those of your race who with unshakable faith summon God to show Himself in the grandiose night of His Name.

You entered into death only to go back to your point of departure. You barely missed the shore. Elya and you became one and the same drowned person.

Your ear, although no longer yours, resisted the void in order to tell you that you were dying.

You entered death with the idea of getting rid of your body and found yourself—O irony—back in your body.

You entered your body, and again, the world seized you.

You will be immodestly nude in the mad love of men.

"I will erase the world," you said, "by painting it in its changing light.

"Thus the face erases the face.

"The stone which resists will learn that it is caught in a universal movement which will transfigure it in spite of itself.

"What will it be tomorrow? Another stone, one it could not have become by itself.

"And I, I am,
"I stay.
"But you, who will you be
"with me, without me, through me, for me?"

> *(Thus God erased Himself in the Other who is*
> *erased.*
> *The eye is doomed.)*

2

You reminded me that the book demands the disbanding of vulgar eyes. To abolish the graven image as the second commandment orders, to reject representation in order to stress the transparency of the word: seen and yet indistinguishable, heard and yet inaudible. The divine word is disquieting smoke. It has never been a blast of strange and terrifying sounds, but a harmonious coiling of a trace burning in the warm air coming down from Sinai. Trace of a trace reverberating in its infinite interdiction.

The voice of day points, proclaims, denounces. It neither renounces itself nor goes beyond. The voice of the dark in forbearing to speak (it does not communicate or, rather, it communicates impossible communication) unearths the sands of the Book of Silence.

This book, Yaël, was our book.

3

> *(Oblivion takes refuge in oblivion.*
> *God emerges from the oblivion of God.*
>
> *"A knot turned into a star?"*
> *"Possibly."*

Oblivion is the bond night cannot untie, but morning cuts.

Oblivion blossoms in the night of oblivion.

A sky full of constellations is a sky of celestial oblivion.

Oblivion, one of the manifestations (the most common) of the void can be defeated only by death. Could the void, at this stage of our evolution, be just the introduction to a beyond which would give us back not only to ourselves, but to the world which we had only half imagined? To lose, to forget all in order to embrace the world of a glance or gesture without ebb.

We owe death a memory which overflows the frame of our lives. We remember what we were before being born as well as what we will have been after ourselves. Because what is at stake but prolonging a reality whose medium we are and which knows that, lit up, it is a match for the day and that, put out, it counts its tracks in the neutral dark?

Thus the chain is never broken. Death verifies the unity.

God does not aspire to be understood, but to be loved. You will never guess why in going towards death you are going towards God. All the riches are bequeathed to you. They are the love of a love without object for which God created the face.

But in order to die you would go as far as stopping to love, as far as loving only absence out of all you love.

Does destroying the face then also mean destroying God? In that case, loving God means above all loving His death.

We start from what is forgotten. The book takes shape from the forgetting of the book.

Oblivion, threads of silver fever, which the night trades with the night. The sky will use them to make the abundant clothes of the sky.

And so a day will break, sewn to an intruding dawn against which the day revolts even now.

Cut the threads, and the world is no more.

Non-writing vies to spread from oblivion to death. The word will come in time to teach it.

Starting from oblivion, I carved a path which death was in favor of. I took the lesson of the second commandment literally. I abolished the world in the word to come. You were dead, Yaël. With you gone, I could advance where you had led and then left me. It was my chance to force the book to close and, reconciling word and step, to glimpse my dead name, your name, Yaël, with its innumerable dry branches.

You talked, devoured by the word kicking in your womb. And your speech was as if beheaded at its birth. What will be built is what was torn from you, easily or with effort.

Ah, how many times did you die for the Book? Killing you, I identified with each of its pages, I appropriated Elya.

> (*Keystone of the vault, key of the void,*
> *Elya: finally the key?*
>
> *After-night of the act. Behind us the night intact.*)

If we never knew who we were, Yaël, it was because we had forgotten. On the other side of the wall stretches the domain of oblivion. We knocked down the obstacle. A past we canceled struggles in our abandoned writings.

The book is always recognition of the book.

(We turned around the abyss, Yaël.
The abyss was your child.)

Hence a stillborn child. Stillborn, that is to say: dead in order to
be born. Life refused even at its birth and stiff at this moment
whose breath and inertia were ours.

Hence a sadistic truth which you gave the manifold face of your
love. I would have been your son without being so, to the point of
drowning in his night in turn. I would have been your lover without
being so, to the point of dying in his skin.

This way we completed the cycle of death, O word to which I
have given hope by throwing it into the chasm. Falling, the flower
perfumes space. On such a persistent scent we will have built our
last dwelling: not a tomb, but the book.

Thus, you could say, on a page-size barry field, there lined up a
secret embryogeny with a bend for words (wing, appendix, bract,
calyx, spur, sepal) which we seized and hastened to destroy. Probably from fear of being read in the unbearable bloom of our sedentary
wanderings.

Once and for all, did we not ransack the garden?

The book really is fire under the axe.

Oblivion, fearful flower plucked at the hour of heaviest sleep. The
bonded screams of the earth mingle with ours when dawn quickens
its colors, when the corolla rivals the solar disk in short-lived beauty.

Any flower has the worth of oblivion.

Equivalence of rites.

Any flower has the warmth of oblivion.

No matter which ritual, death will never be solemnized. This way
we completed the voyage around death, O word to which I have
given the hope of being, someday, forgotten.

This way my unchecked gesture (thought about, though, in its
dark imperative) and your lucid, desperate behavior join and vie for

the same privilege of setting the book in its foundation. Not to be taken in by a planned word, but to be accomplices of its internal contradictions. The agony of speech is the coming of the word. The book is written at the expense of life, at the cost of flesh.

"And to dust thou shalt return . . ." Writing: personification and confirmation of dust.

> *(Fraternal tedder, which the blind man claims at the edge of the field.*
> *Between life and death you wait for a blasted glance—a blasted love—to which the day answers.)*

It is this day threatened by night, Yaël, which held the gem of your youth, star of priceless radiance.

You died in the sun by my will. We were at the same time the past hour, year, and century.

Once dead, eternity reveled in the irrational and ridiculous stands we had made.

Elya, you, and I: we were only haphazard distortions of a shadow before total darkness.

Night is a gigantic collective conquest. In the sky, there gleam the golden tips of the flags of oblivion.

Door III
(An Afternoon in the Luxembourg Gardens)

A book like a series of doors. Only the passage from one to the next is to be spoken, to be read.

1

We speak to what is blossoming. What listens is shedding its leaves.

I was walking towards the Luxembourg Gardens, with a book under my arm. A warm and sunny afternoon. I was thinking of the questions I had been asked the night before by the representative of a literary weekly. I was trying to reassemble my statements in my mind, not, to be sure, to modify them—it was too late for that—but because I had answered carelessly which is not my habit. I reproached myself for this interview, as I often reproach myself for the most harmless confidences.

I am only—the moment confirms it—a man of writing, that is to say, a man who keeps his secret faced with a word. I am not eager to express myself. I expose myself to the sometimes poisonous pricks of my pen. And as if my body suddenly existed only to undergo this ordeal. Whether chasm or sky, the formation of words leaves gaping wounds. In them the worlds feel at ease. Each evolves in its area, ignoring the others. This ignorance is my main reason for writing.

To teach the universe to know itself by making myself into one wound. Whether bond or erasure, the space between words is equally night or morning. Unity is supreme suffering. One and the same flesh, one poor soul in shreds.

(There is no exile outside time.
My people is the people of the present tense.)

It would be enough, after all, to save the glance in order to make the All appear in its indissolubility.

Formidable adventure of the mind, O most formidable: to open the night to the night.

The whole of night was our reading.

(My people is One in suffering.)

Let oblivion then be only one more step.

2

A little girl sang:
"In the ocean dormitory,
as many boarders as you wish.
A man's dreams can never
rival the dreams of fish."

My memory is an old horseshoe. Ah, gallop off, my four memories.

I am a rider without mount, an ocean without waves, a horizon without dawn,

nailed to myself, nailed to an absence in time which, after me, becomes the time of absence.

The little girl sang:
"Inside the cemetery
were seven children's bones.
Six of them were earth.
The tallest one was stone."

You can speak only on this side of death, in this tormented eternity which is the last but one existence of eternity. Silence envelops life. Hail, most kind, most dear, most gentle refuge where God is without birth.

3

I give up. I give my tongue to the dogs.

Bark, pack let loose. The hunt is raging.
In dying, we carry the world along into the void.
Myriads of stars cover us, flowers fallen from everywhere.
Thus the sky forms anew, in death, for love of a man become immense through the grace of love.

Yesterday, the void. Tomorrow, the nothing. Nobody had told us that there are doors scattered through space, and that they are condemned in advance.

"A failure, isn't it?" he had said.

"A failure, indeed," I had answered.

I think I have nothing more to say about this quest.
We will turn from the seed page.

At the end of your thoughts, you are so small that you no longer have the looks of a man, nor any age.

How the dead look alike.

The flesh is the miracle of a bright moment when desire seizes the creature.

The world is not enough for God
or us.

The failure overwhelms us.

God has plunged into the word where I too plunge to come to His aid.

A bottomless hole, I tell you. Once the center of a universe stricken by blindness to which all roads led.

Elya had disowned his mother
before she knew.

4

A policeman's whistle. Closing time. Adults and children calling. Laughs and screams all around. Will there be an exit for me? I keep aloof inside my eyeballs. I too become a marble statue. My white eyes widen and swallow the garden. I glide on the wave. No more need to speak. It is words that outline our limits.

The wind. The open sea. Ah, that their rage could carry off our ruins.

How many dead in death. How much forgetting in oblivion.

The challenge of the book is a challenge of silence.

Door IV
(The Disciple)

The book is the vague consciousness of going beyond yourself, the need for which will show only later.

To wait, in the shade of time, for the time to come, the time which, tomorrow, will be ours and where, again, the consoled word will nestle against the word.

Eternity of the flower in its last homage.
O Yaël, immortal for making death flower.

1

"I followed you. You had nothing to offer but emptiness, in other words, nothing."

"The emptiness inside every being and every thing, yes. We will have ploughed through the world at the heart of a word we had to destroy."

"I followed you faithfully along your road in the burning sun. We could not even count on Yaël's shadow to ease our rest."

"I have not known any rest in my quest of the absolute. What madmen we are. And I do not know your face."

"Neither do I know yours. Are you *the other*? When you speak to me, are you the incarnation of Yaël?"

"Yaël will not come to life in the book."

"Have we been the book?"

"Perhaps we have been the moment when the book turns on its thirst."

"But who would have opened it, this book? How did we enter, caught in our own trap? And for what reading have we been alphabet?"

"What use to worry about our daring? Man will forever be read. The question writes us."

2

"Excuse me, sir . . . I would like you to meet Alain, who wanted to see you. He might someday ask you questions about your books.

"It's about Elya . . . you know. What coincidence.

"Alain had entered into silence. Suddenly he recognized himself in Elya.

"A stillborn child, what an odd image of oneself. But he is not dead, my son isn't. He may be silent, but he is quite alive. He breathes. He moves. He grows taller every year. He is only eighteen, but he could easily pass for twenty-two, don't you think?

"I will leave you two alone. I have to go.

"Provided that he will talk, good God, provided that he will be able to tell you what he ruminates on so distantly and what eats him. A real camel . . . but camels are not restless. He is too much so.

"A desert creature, that's it. He never asks anything. He waits. He hardly walks, eats, or drinks. He writes when he feels like it. He presents himself like a book to be deciphered. Most of the time, a forbidden book.

"What are you going to do to get him to open up? When I told him: 'I know the author of *Elya*,' he looked at me, put his notebook aside, and plunged into your book as if trying to take his rightful place there and to keep it for good.

"He was transformed. It was then I decided to bring him here. I shouted '*Elya*,' and he smiled. But he was at the bottom of your pages.

"I come as it were with your book. I have not read it, I am sorry. But every day I bend over my son to try and discover the secret of his silence. And in those moments, I perhaps read one of your chapters inadvertently. As a beggar. In despair.

"Forgive me. My son is my unquenchable love. His warmth, his gentleness are vital for me. I cannot stand to be cut off from him. He is my fireplace, my well of water.

"I thought that faced with his stubborn silence, faced with your work, you could . . . you would know the right gesture, find the words which would bring him back to me. Because it is not going to be Alain who will ever talk, but you with his voice, driven from the book by the book; you in pursuit of a less cruel truth which will leave my son to his youth, leave him to me.

"What are you thinking, sir? You do not answer me either.

"Elya has become my son. I have not deserved such a fate.

"I know you can with a stroke of your pen change the state of things. Alain would recognize me. I am his mother. His real mother. Alain is my son, and I have stood by his life from the first scream that burst from his little, red chest.

"I am losing my courage and the strength to skirt death without help.

"How quiet it is, suddenly. I am the only one to talk, and I cannot hear my words.

"There we are, you, me, and my son, and nothing moves, nothing happens between us. A word by itself in the air is a soap bubble.

"Elya died for my son and revealed to him his own death of which we are in vain taking inventory.

"I shall wait. Sometime the universe will have to brighten and to express itself as a whole.

"But what do you want to know, sir, that you do not know already?

"I, for my part, expect nothing from this knowledge which leads to the silence of a truth with God as its end, nor from words without echo.

"My son is here, alive. Elya is a humble lamp turned off. We cannot resist long in the dark. Unless the blackness is our eternity.

"My flesh claims my son. Had you thought for even one moment that Alain, your most exemplary disciple, could have a mother?

"Destroy the book by destroying yourself. Kill my son in death in order to save his life. We will be reborn, all three.

"Then the word will have sense and the world a name."

The young man did not take his eyes off me. Alain really had the lucid stubbornness of words. What was he hoping for? No doubt that I would return to the book which he had not renounced, that he would remain its reality, and I its attempt.—But was he aware that he excluded me from each sentence by taking them all on himself?

With him, the book was gliding into the silence of a death which heeded only its own sinuous course as if we were but an embarrassing and small moment of our impotent sleep, a wrenching and wrenched moment of our eyes blasted on opening. Thus everything would continue to happen inside sight where the book answers to the book, where God can be approached and perceived. And everything would arrange itself in a free, but precise order.

I lowered my eyes, I think I even shut them. I had become again the prey of Elya and had to vouch for the life and liberty of this young man whom a tearful mother for the second time forced me to question.

What do you want of me? Silence has only one confidant: Silence.

I killed the word, and it stealthily rose again under the features of a strange woman.

I did not find you in her, Yaël. But her child was indeed your son.

(Death does not share.)

AELY
VOLUME VI

"Do you know that the final period of the book is an eye," he said, "and without lid?"

Dieu, "God," he spelled *D'yeux*, "of eyes." "The 'D' stands for desire," he added. "Desire to see. Desire to be seen."

God resembles His Name to the letter, and His Name is the Law.

BEFORE THE FORE-BOOK I

Your law is just. You have listened to the book.

In the spiralings before the fore-book you discover, along with the broken circle, that the center is also the peak.

The eye is the most towering abyss.

The law of the book is law of the abyss.

He said: "*Justice* and *Loi*, 'Law,' have one vowel in common. This letter is their only link. It is also found in the word *Bien*, 'Good.'
"*Mal*, 'Evil,' shares a consonant with *Loi*. Both Good and Evil ripen in the shadow of the Law. But Justice only sides with Good."
He also said: "God is not good. He is good writing."

We do not know the law of the book because nobody knows what good is; but we innocently practice it by writing.

The "o" of the word *Loi* is its chasm, its center. There is the chasm of Good and the chasm of Evil. But where is their center?

"The 'o' of the word *Loi* is a wheel," he said.
"Can the wheel of law be compared to that of fortune? Apparently not . . . except that both yearn
for justice."

In the book, voice and faith, *voix* and *foi*, are
parallel roads, parallel furrows in the law.

Divine day is the day when nobody sees. Day
before writing, perhaps, day of the blank page.
He said: "Prisoner of the page, God's suffering is
mine."
Divine day is the writer's first hour.
Hell. Hell.

Between the furrows, the far side of death.

1

You are there. You look around. Are you at the beginning?

An eye, young again where all is done with, looks at you.

Yukel dead.

Sarah and Yaël dead.

After Elya,

who is Aely? He is oblivion, I said. Oblivion of the scarred, disemboweled woman crushed by her stillborn child. Oblivion of the world, oblivion of life and the void.

The eye of all that has not been.

"Do we see other beings and things because they see us?" he asked. "Then all discovery is only the point where two looks meet.

"Then seeing is more than receiving, much more than perceiving the object through our eyes: it means recognizing an appeal by its secret desire, and answering it."

In the beginning, the look is ever proof and test of a love.

Laws of the visible and invisible. You hesitate. You feel your way. You do not know that you put into words the laws of life and death.

Unawares, the writer has been chosen to formulate the law.

The law was at first the writing of rocks. We approach it as the rock of writing. The book is the potstone of the book. The law is the fire.

"A book," he said, "is also an earthenware bowl fired by the sun. From it you drink the vastness of the world. But do not think that it will always quench your thirst. Its brew is most often bitter."

He said:
"Chance is a pearl of chaos, a priceless trump secreted by the shell."
And he added:
"Any word is a challenge to chance."

"If, in the space where the book forms, eye and ear are at the mercy of chance," he asked, "is this not because chance is also at the mercy of eye and ear?"

Necessity, in the book, is what is born, has ceased to be, and is cited by death.

What you expect from the book is perhaps what it expects from you. Then writing would be the double complicity with an overriding desire to be realized in the book—at the expense of every word with which you have identified, i.e., at the expense of your life.

The highest ambition of writing would then be the desperate attempt to experience its death.

The book's question is innocent.

You will turn chance into a yeast of questions.

2

(*We cannot be seized before the word, before the gesture, only after. But in the silence which follows we again, alas, are unseizable.*

Oblivion means birth.)

From the promontory above the city I looked out on the sea.

I watched one wave pull another to its end, assist it in its impending agony, then return to its point of departure—but perhaps it was no longer the same wave?—to get another wave and force—or help—it to die in turn.

You could have said that these waves, which died under an impassive sky, at the edge of the water, announced themselves by their death or, rather, by the color they took on as they approached their end. The most daring were white and surrendered to the sand as if they had come to meet a distant death, a death at the end of all deaths, incomprehensible to reason.

Complex games, graceful in their cruelty where chance seemed to play an important part. But was it not all fixed in advance?

Let us assume an infinite number of vague, unquestioned laws derived from the Law, yet defying it, dependent on it and constituting both its strength and weakness. The unmanageable, the unexpected, for example, would then have their laws as much as life, the dream with its aggressive peaks or gentle slopes, and death. Occult laws, appropriate to this time of truce, of the Law napping; time over which the Law has no direct hold, but which it might, after inspired consideration, use to enlarge its empire; time underground and on the night side of the Law where it reserves an option to probe the unknowable.

("I love you for all that is born," Yukel wrote to Sarah. "I forget who you are so that I can discover you with the moment and die of you.")

A starfish was lying on the sand. The beach had saved it for me. Already dry, out of its depth of translucent ink where it had grown, gelatinous. Already dead, dead from the start perhaps for loving the sun too much. A star: this is the point to surrender my writing. Was the book written then? It remained this dry and hard eye, this mute questioning of the book.

BEFORE THE FORE-BOOK II

"You must know that even a glimmer in its very paleness is already law," he said.

The Threshold of Glimmers

In the silence of life, in the shredded book.

"In the book," he said, "writing means absence, and the empty page, presence.
"Thus God, who is absence, is present in the book."

Emptiness become law.
The open book.

Image of balances.
The trays are pages.
Weight of the word. But what weight silence?

On one tray of the scales, silence, on the other, silence also.

In writing we give proof of submission to the law, submission to God, submission to emptiness.

"Man is a decumbent stem," he said.
"Our desire for change is often only a repressed need to undo a previous change."

An eye catches and leads me astray.
Though seen, I cannot see myself.

The book, disclosed in its far-off parts.

I am not haunted by the center, but by con-
centricity where the book, in every phase of its
evolution, unwittingly circles its death.

God, an obliterating tyrant? World and man perish where the Word rages.
Our words testify above all to divine obliteration.

Last whirl of water
over the submerged wreck.
White eye,
monstrous, fearful
on the calm surface.
Absent eye, eye of harrowing,
unbearable absence.

Purity, limpidity can only be described to the
transparent. Air is told to a breath of air, water to
the drop.

Almost all.
Almost nothing.
Only in the void can we be all and nothing.
We will almost have lived, almost known death.

The hand also writes the invisible.

The Threshold of the Eye

Within the word *oeil*, "eye," there is the word *loi*, "law." Every look contains the law.

A book—and dying words entertain you with the immortality of the Creator and created.

"God is the future of death," he said. "However, future means life.

"I imagine a body so inviolable that it would last forever, but death wastes the body first. Does waste take the place of the future? This would mean that God reproduces Himself out of His sacrificed Totality, that is, out of the boldness of Nothing. Schizogenetic void which braves the void in the name of an emptiness as dizzying as the universe and which is, if not God, at least His immortality."

"God's absence is immortal," he had jotted down one day, "and God only the reference to this immortality."

1

"Writing," he said, "is the universe drawn on the scale of the book."

. . . one law, tablet of marble or burned wood, one law for life and death.

One law, like an eye within the law, the incorruptible eye of the letter. To observe the law to the letter—does this not mean keeping firmly within your field of vision?

Suppose that God was never anything but the future and past of a book, an eye, a sign, and, especially, the four erased letters of His name.

One law for God—as if God were the Law—therefore one Law for the Law.

One law for man in quest of God.

The meeting of God and man cannot be imagined without the mediating word, but continues in its silence.

Law which governs the relations of day and day, of night and night, of moment and moment, of eternity and eternity of which the white page is the fierce repository.

I say that this law of the book is Jewish.

I say that this law of God in the book is Jewish.

I say that this law of man in the book is Jewish because every letter in the book is the skeleton of a Jew.

2

You turn black, black in death where all is white.

(God chose death in order to live and gave man life so he should die. The latter expects his end from the word, the Former His resurrection.

Writing is followed and heard up to the point where it stops being writing and becomes the deep sense of a passionate deletion.

Wherever we go, whatever we do, whichever trick we try to escape our condition, we are seen, we

are looked at, and will never know by whom or why,
nor with what right or to what end.)

"Do not think walls can keep you apart," he said. "They are
pierced by an eye which belongs to no one."
Eye of a world without God or of God without the world?
O you who have come and stayed.
O you who were here, but are no more.
An eye remembers and awakens my memory. An eye like a sheath
for the One—primordial figure, Unity, Totality of God—to slide in,
a rod in attack. O Marriage-wound. O regeneration of God in His
first divine act. Only God could conceive God. Eye to the left of the
One, having come first: empty eye in the shape of an "o," zero and
simplistic sign which divides Unity while taking form and then, on
the right, multiplies it to the infinite. First, chaos, matrix, vagina,
then planet, space, universe, but always a void, active or passive,
bright emptiness.
Would God, expelled from the hole, gravitate towards Zero?
We will have seen how absence is born and borne away. Thus men
pass and pass away, and God within man, from word to word, from
figure to figure.
The stakes of death: God become word.
You know through the book how and where you will die.
You have this certainty so that God can exist.

(*"Good is pure avowal, Evil beyond words,"* he
said.)

The Threshold of the Void

   . . . perhaps the unproven certainty of a law, a
merciless law,
   the law of Good in the swamps of Evil.
   The book is not built, but unbuilt. God dies of
the book.
   The book, bottomless tomb of God?
   This unbuilding means a return to the initial
word.
   Basic law of the space before night, both dark
and light scatter its principle to the winds.
   An architect's blueprint shows through the white
sheet.
   The writer builds his house in the invisible and
immediately destroys it so it can be everybody's
house forever.
   Does the dark let us read the stars, and the
splayed light the roots? Then the law of the book is
the law of the infinite, law of what has always been
empty, law of hospitality and silence.

The route of writing goes through the night. Will other eyes see
for us where we can no longer see? We are never lost.

"It is incontrovertible," he said, "that summer is the eye of the
seasons."

"It is doubtful," he also said, "that the star sees the pebble, but,
on the other hand, certain that the pebble sees the star."

(The dark, which God burdened with His crea-
tion, is again blank on awakening.

In the morning, you tear up the pages of your
fever, but every word naturally leads you back to
its color, its night.

Morning counts its dead, enumerates the lined-
up words of our differences.
Day is edged with mourning.

"God," he said, "is the harrowing reply to the
posthumous accusations of Creation."

"If you bend over your page," he said, "and do
not suddenly tremble with fear, throw away your
pen. Your writing would have little value.")

THE FORE-BOOK I

Any voice hoists itself home and pollards itself in the neighborhood of a voice.

"You bathe—O transparency—in the literalness of the book as in a calm and clear bay, and you will drown there. This also is just," he said.

(. . . *a voice perhaps—mine?—perhaps only the ghost of a voice, of a word. Perhaps a few words from a word so lonely that it slips away from both the I and the You. Word of a different absence, a stranger even to absence; word of a different silence, both sap and thirst of silence. Perhaps just the inkling of a word coming after the word, after even the after-word. Like a ring, but for which finger? Like a watch, but to give whom the time? Like a dewdrop, but on which flower? Like a bit of salt water, but cupped from which ocean? A word coiled up in its voice, useless, useless except for the voice, for the uncertain burial of an unseen word.*
Aely's voice and word.)

Nowhere

The word remains objective where subjectivity afflicts us.

Truth is objective.
The law is objective.
Death is objective.
We must think of God as an objective Totality.

He said: "Am I the man God did not recognize? If so I have done searching. For me, God is nowhere."

1

A look cut off from any eye, any being, any god. A look over which neither life nor death has any hold, a look where the end of day and the end of night miscarry.

Abyss within a deeper abyss, void within a vaster void. A look beyond looking, which sees where no eyes see, which has engulfed them, one after another, at the height of their power. An unobliging look, beyond attention, beyond chance, beyond abandon, and whose strength is the more formidable for being anonymous: the look of All and Nothing.

This look, we now know, has followed us everywhere. We salute it as we enter our death.

(Look of Sarah, of Yukel, of the stillborn child,
Elya.
In work after work, I have lucidly given in to
this look,
helpless, alone in Aely's retinal field.)

2

God alone knows His image.

Before the Creation, God could expect everything of God, just as the writer can expect everything of his pen before the book, and the book
everything of the book before it is written.
. . . this expectation, however, is due to the
creator not knowing himself, nor the book knowing the book.
We build on ignorance and build our ruin.

Before the Creation, God is All. Afterwards, ah, is He Nothing
afterwards?
The All is invisible. Visibility lies between All and Nothing, in
each little bit taken from the All.
In order to create, God went outside Himself so that he could
penetrate and destroy Himself.
When He had created the world, God was All without heaven
and earth.
When He had created day and night, God was All without the
stars.
When He had created animals and vegetation, God was All
without the fauna and flora of the globe.
When he had created man, God was without face.
Nobody has seen God, but the stages of His death are visible
to all of us.

*(The word will start from Nothing in order to
dissolve in the All.
Likewise any law.)*

3

Life and creation breathe the same breath.

What does not allow any answer keeps the question awake forever.

All inquiry is yoked to the eyes. O impossible question of God.

God, the uncreated, that is, created before God, being where
nothing exists.
God, the creator and hence destroyer of God,
because the All had to show proof of its innate Totality as it faced
the void, down to the final stripping where victim and hangman embrace and sink into baffling absence.

Tackling each knot in turn, we have tied ourselves to the task of
untangling the threads of our origins. O redeemed silence, base of
the book.

Worshiping the invisible God, the Jew lifted his gaze to its
apogee where the imperative word chooses to become legible
commandment.

God taught us that writing is eternal, at the eyes' farthest reach.

The book sees for all its words.

4

In the kingdom of sand, a sound promises eyes.

In order to see Himself, God chose to speak in the desert.

Because God is immortal, death is immortal likewise.

Writing

> Throw yourself into the sea.
> You will hear God.
> Dig into the desert.
> God will hear you.
> Only death can hear
> death.

You could have said a tide of sounds, varying from the lowest to the most piercing, was advancing on the beach, besieging it.

I briefly thought that, one day, sounds would make me the master of language and the sea.

How could I have guessed that through their accord or rivalry death appropriates the word, and that the letters composing it indulge, while carving its meaning into the rock, in murmuring a daring, but airtight explanation of our common end whose secret stages they anticipate.

. . . A murmuring so soft that I have not ever heard it.

The image of a fisher's hut on fire, by the sea, near the rock I used to sit on, dazzling spectacle of the determined though spontaneous dialogue of fire and fire which went on in spite—or perhaps because—of the wind and which was suddenly stopped by a huge leap of a wave—this image quickly became exemplary for me and confirmed my conviction that an undatable death, both alien and familiar, lies in wait for any death and rules over man and world.

We write dreading this death.

Once you know this you already possess one of the keys to the book, and the least accessible.

("*The tide, gigantic cam, daily completes its high-warp tapestry,*" he said.

"*It may happen that a nearby fire gets caught in it for a fleeting deposit of gold thread which the tide had dreamed of stealing from the sun.*")

A Glimpse of the Book

An approach. Sketch of a gesture.
Shivering nudity.
O apprehension of rocks.
Mad desire, winged desire, diamond-laden desire of man.

It seems that all that is essential for me is born of the well-tried, banal idea that the act of seeing fuses with the secret desire to be seen.

Does it also hold that we see and are seen in the void? The word seems to bear this out.

Then there is a death which looks at death deferring entirely to its look.

Where am I? At a point when I do not yet know the book. O enticing liquid sweep. I walk along the shore. The moment will come when I plunge in, a bold swimmer. But only for a while. Then I get paralyzed and promptly go down.

Image of the writer: a drowned man washed up on the shore. He has seen the bottom of the sea which is also the deepest desire. O truth coiled on itself. The writer has only had the merest glimpse of the book, but paid for it with his life.

Hence any plausible account of writing must start with death. With the released memory of time.

. . . The sign calls the void to account at this turn of the hour when the ripped dawn forever opposes the world to the world.

The book of knowledge is a book off the ledge of night.

The writer answers for his glimpse of the book which the book ratifies in death.

> *(Birth is the consummate moment when death is gone from the heart of death.*
>
> *Thus an absence within absence could be a perpetual beginning.*
>
> *Could this be God?*
>
> *. . . God, the Absent, but beyond the power of absence, hence bound to be present where all presence is revoked?)*

Absence within presence, presence within absence. Seeing is God's superb challenge which man in his pride accepts in order to be His equal.

If living means seeing, then dying must mean being seen.

Then life and death are only the double adventure lived by the eye.

Dark, propitious to reason, O night of glistening snares which the soul crosses, unswerving, like a comet.

Flame flung at flame.

God, who is at the center of all meditation, so despises Thought that the latter cannot think itself in Him and thus vainly exhausts itself trying to feed its fire.

A hothouse plant, thought blossoms and wilts alone.

If I am because I think, my solitude is infinite.

The book is a solitude of sand where every word leaves an imprint of its voice.

You read in silence what once was said by all.

The eye is absence opening its lid.

THE FORE-BOOK II

"From here on, the book takes the place left empty by the last one. A thousand ears of wheat follow as many before them."

"Could it be that, like a farmer his field, you have ploughed silence from one book to the next?"

"Before and after the words we always worry about silence, its arid soil."

Is the noise in the sea or the sea in the noise?
Rock, bastion of stillness.
Will the noise drown out silence?
The sea wear down the rock?

God warrants the disappearance of God as the word warrants man's complicity with death. Thus God and man join the streamlined furrows of the immaculate page.

Is death what resists me, what escapes me? Then how come I die with full hands?

Water makes a furrow to prove it can break with the water.

In the Furrows of the Fore-Book I

Writing is not man's projection, but it traces his devotion to the void. It becomes the record of his negativity.

The book is made against the book, just as a word in a dialogue opposes the word which engendered it.

Does the task of composing a book consist in letting the dialogue develop freely within it?

Death spies on death. We could not dispute this.

Then margins are that portion of silence which two voices compete for.

An answer bears the weight of the question it rejects or continues. In fact, the answer is contained in its question which does not know this.

The answer is allotted the space left behind by the question. Either the answer offsets the question, i.e., becomes a reply to its own inquiry in order to go the rest of the way alone, or it leaves the question to its impatience to know, forcing it just to mark time.

The path of the question, as mapped by the answer, leads straight to death, which is always the first question.

The question, butt for the answer's refusal, breaks us on the threshold of the void.

It is in this sense that the writer is a stranger: on the road to death or at the edge of the precipice.

In the purer night towards which the words climb, a book which has survived all will join the dawn.

This book will not have our voice. Neither will it speak to us. In spite of the distance, it will continue its dialogue with the books littering its path and whose silence has always haunted it.

(*Voices of silence, who could know you? Mine comes back to me where nothing and no one exists.*

We die against death. O boundaries, prey of the boundless.

Let me die with my face buried in sand. The inscrutable sky avenges us on oblivion.)

In the Furrows of the Fore-Book II

1

A life without furrows is not even a sigh. It is a death unmenaced by any term.

You cross death in the dark or illuminated.
Did you know that in death, tiers of dark and light rise to the infinite?
Thus the dead are never at the same level of severance in this empty space.

The loss of consciousness which supposedly characterizes our state in death is an additional hoax. The book is glaring proof of it.
The dead are as lucid as the living, but cannot be pinned down.
They no longer own their faces.
Any face is their face.
Any word their name.

To see to the point where the world stops being visible. Go and look farther, but despair of seeing anything. Death quenches our thirsty lives beyond all life. Our houses are of ashes, of black night and ashes.

Does dying mean, in the book, becoming invisible for everyone else, but decipherable to yourself?

The book enumerates our steps inside death.

. . . But did this God reason like a man of the Letter?
Obsessed with the Book, He married its words. For He knew that
each of them bore a question which He should be careful to restore
to silence.

Every book falls silent with God.

2

Has the time come for me to face the questions of my books?
As if I should, at least with them, accept responsibility for having
written them
when it seems to me that I have none, when, on the contrary, in
my heart of hearts I accuse them of having traded my life for another
which I find hard to live.
But perhaps they are calling me to account precisely for this latter
existence which I owe them?
In this case, my books question my books across me.

> (*Thus, without ever stepping outside the silence
> he explores, Aely has taken Elya's place in Yaël's
> utterances.*
>
> *The supreme interrogation—O rout of the spirit
> —is when emptiness questions emptiness, and the
> universe is afraid.*
>
> *Aely, book open to books.*)

Twin mirrors of emptiness. The image of the book is what the facing pages reflect back and forth.

. . . Also, he took pains to show that there are major works (one or two in a century) which are majestically turned towards ours, critical eyes fixed on all that is—or is to be—written. One day our books will die at their feet.

But, he quickly added, these works are not the same for every generation of writers. Which allowed him to conclude—maybe too hastily—that it is our work which opens their eyes.

(Death has always been the Jew's discreet confidant, the humble mirror in which, every night, in the same spot, by a candle, he scrutinizes his face.)

Where the Word Answers to the Name Yaël

1

What is surprising about the word one day claiming a body, a body and a soul by insisting on a name?

But was this woman in whom the word wanted to be embodied merely a woman?

Silence molded her, and she offered herself by unraveling this silence as death pursued her.

Dead since, she belongs to me only in death, which prefigured our union and solemnly consecrated it.

When I, in turn, ceased to be in order to become indefinitely *the other* in her desire to annihilate me, the book spread from horizon to horizon.

We cannot reach full, perfect understanding with ourselves.

Any gesture confronts us with the destructiveness of gestures, O deceitful laments.

We shall no longer judge ourselves by our actions, but by the hideous gash.

. . . But was this woman in whom the word wanted to be embodied merely a woman? She held that the body is joined to the body by numerous bridges, and that in life as in death we linger on one or the other of its banks, left or right. She argued from the fact that when I ceased to be in order to become indefinitely *the other* in her desire to destroy me, love drew its strength from death and needed the sacrifice of my face in order to blossom. She took pleasure in claiming that, between us, we embodied all the passion of the world, exclusive passion which mocks boundaries and shakes the living as much as the dead.

Space is first of all within us. Death is a revelation of space.

An unsteady distance separates flesh from flesh, spirit from spirit, senses from senses, just as it has separated water from water, sand from sand, our planet from other planets. A seemingly passive distance whose fluctuating movement and internal activity she had nevertheless sensed.

Soon this distance became our main preoccupation. Our lives, our deaths took place within its confines which we tried to widen beyond ourselves. One more try and we would have broken down for good.

This will to live within death, as strong as that which quickens truth in its fight against the lie and sometimes pushes it to use the enemy's weapons—does enduring not mean surviving self and world by any means?—this will to grow, to love, to procreate within death was the prelude to an extraordinary adventure. "A search for harmony," she said, but it was because the word had suddenly fallen in love with silence and our blood was the price.

> (*O Yaël, in one single gush your blood, mingled*
> *with mine, sealed the feast.*
> *The heart beats with light.*
>
> "*Shed blood*," *she confided to me,* "*is the sadistic*
> *light of death.*")

2

Blood fertilizes, perpetuates.

The eye: blood's hoisted trophy.

("It happens," he said, "when I am preoccupied by a thought, that I unwittingly turn away from it to concentrate on other thoughts that have arisen in the meantime.

"Developing a thought means first of all the death of this thought for the benefit of another, which chance or its own strict requirements raised in order to strike it down in turn.

"O sinuous, serpentine paths of the conscious mind's inheritance. O complex mechanism of knowledge.

"Our way is paved with rival thoughts, each of them a dazzling moment of Thought.

"It could be that truth and thought are only sublime metamorphoses of nothing."

"The tree of Knowledge," he added, "is, after all, the tree of Death."

. . . Out of the "in-between" caused by the unexpected reversal of a thought without mirrors, thought rises again to ripen and die in its time, like the one before, all so that death can continue thinking itself.

The irrevocable order of Creation was established under the law of balance; balance revealing the play of antagonisms where water is defined by the fire which burns it and which it quenches, dark by the light which it blinds and in which it lies down exhausted, good by the evil which mines and exalts it.

To violate this law means for the spring to run dry in its spring, for the eye to lose the glow of the eye, for matter to be strangled by matter, and hence, making the original unity of the world inconceivable, i.e., invisible.

Death, to which they are led facing their final
phase, would then be the sum of our contradictions
systematically canceled out by one another
and God, His absurd absence.)

"It is in exile and pain," Yaël had noted, "that we see clearly what
had long remained hidden. No veil can obstruct the uprooted eye
whose every tear on this dark slope of life glistens like a drop of water fallen from a star,
glitter by glitter."

THE FORE-BOOK III

One letter dropped from your name, and already you are no more.

1

. . . this is why I dreamed of a work which would not enter into any category, fit any genre, but contain them all; a work hard to define, but defining itself precisely by this lack of definition; a work which would not answer to any name, but had donned them all; a work belonging to no party or persuasion; a work of earth in the sky and of sky on earth; a work which would be the rallying point of all the words scattered in space whose loneliness and discomfiture we do not suspect; the place beyond all place of an obsession with God, unquenched desire of a mad desire; a book, finally, which would only surrender by fragments, each of them the beginning of another book.

Book, object of an inexhaustible quest. Is this not how the Jewish tradition sees the Book?

"The words which rise to our lips," he said, "have come to us from the bottom of the ages.
"We repeat them for the times to come."

Words that cannot be heard: a desert.

The Eternal: Gods fused into God.

("A search for harmony," she had said at the crossroads where we were drawn and quartered by our contradictions.
And she had added: ". . . at every instant of the book, which is a vibrant mirror of death."

Nothing is lost. Even trial words and gestures are collected and preserved by death.

O Yaël, in the dark, down with the roots, the one-day flower blooms forever.)

2

What am I committed to?—The necessity of the book.

The book is alone before the unknown, the writer in the solitude of the book.
Flint in the desert.

To split open a stone. To polish carefully the smooth surfaces brought to light.
A fatal wound has turned the stone into a book.
Ah, who but ourselves can perform this miracle on us at the hour of our death?

You attribute things to me which are not in the book, things you think you have guessed. So I am baited by what it expresses against my will and by what you retain.

Life gets only one portion of the book's inheritance: the poor man's portion.

All my life I shall have taken up the scent of a word which patiently, stubbornly led me to my death.
Thus the Jew dies for his name.

"What is your name?"
"Look at my face."

"What is your name?"
"Look at my hands."

"What is your name?"
"Look at the road."

In the maze of signs, the beyond is the harrowing plea of our origins, noticed from one dawn to the next.

Morning was our last halt.

3

"I am not called Aely. Nobody has given me this name. It is the name of a book. Am I this book? I can only be so in so far as it is the deciphered silence of a name,
 "so that we support each other in similar and pathetic absence.
 ". . . But this absence cannot be evoked.
 "I have no life and never had one.
 "I do not exist.
 "I escape all that escapes me, escapes you,
 "you who talk,
 "who pursue me,
 "who die."

Voice from the far side of silence, ah, how clear it was here.

> ("Aely," I repeated, "Aely, the elsewhere of an
> unimaginable elsewhere,
> seed of silence."

Dreaming is above us, silence below, in stones.

"Sky, earth, and sea are contained in stone,"
he said, "and on the scales of the universal bal-
ance, it is the measuring unit of silence.")

4

A man of writing is a man of the four letters which form the unpronounceable Name. God is absent through His Name.

Writing means taking on God's absence through each of the four.

Thus any page of writing is fashioned under the sign of four letters which are the masters of its fate, with power to make it disappear through the expedient of the words containing them.

Absence is everywhere, ready to surprise us in the most dynamic or harmless word.

However, those four letters are not alone in distilling absence.

Any word which eludes the meaning bent on fixing it is free in terms of an absence which is its freedom to live and die, towards which it has always gravitated,

. . . in terms of an uncertain space whose horizon is the four letters of silence.

(Words lose their transparency in being read.
Passage of the silvered glass into the mirror.
There are words which remain mirrors even
without silvering.

Does choice take the place of silver? Does the
word choose its death?

"Death," said Yaël, "is reading.")

5

Trembling I advance in the book whose every
word can cause a quake.

I have always felt a strange, vague presence near me: shadowy
at night, a paler whiteness in the day, and changing shapes to the
point of having none at the moments when I feared it most.
Fascinated, I found myself at a crossroad; but in front of a hole.
There, night and day did not know each other. I approached a
death which did not know death because it had not known life, a
death without dead, an orphaned life without lives,
where nothing was ever other than nothing.

. . . My intuition had not deceived me. Somewhere in death,
there is a place where any place we have reached disappears,
where its disappearance is noted without, for all that, being taken
in charge.

Have we practiced drawing lines around what will never be
written because not felt or thought?

"The ambiguity of this death," he said, "is indeed that of God."
. . . But what if night thought it could also be day, and day
likewise night?

6

*(I am ousted by my books and, little by little,
called back. Then I know I am about to write a
new book or, rather, my other books are ready to
take turns dictating it to me, and my hand will
obey.*
Can I ever get out?
Prisoner of my first word, my first work, which, I

am now convinced, were aware that they contained
all the others. Therefore I sometimes look at them
with awe.

The word is dreamed by the letter, and the book
by the fabulous dreams of the word.

Was this all I attempted: circling the vastest
word, the first one to be watered by my ink?

My books would bear this out. They witness to
my tireless wandering through the night of a word
both indifferent and possessive

where nothing is asked of the witness.

—But which is this word? Perhaps I have not yet
written it.)

The Empty Notebook

Have I been reading without matter, reading an empty notebook?

Is departing this life simply an imprudent change of place?
You die of yourself as you have lived on yourself.

A stubbed silence relentlessly disturbs silence.

"If you believe in emptiness," he said, "you must believe in infinite emptiness, and infinite emptiness is God, the dizzying place of the book."

"You are . . ."
"No doubt, but . . ."
"So you are the person to . . ."
"Probably, but . . ."
"You seem hesitant."
"Well, I am not sure I can answer you."
"But this is you; this *is* your name."
"Yes, certainly . . . but it's something else."
"What?"
"I don't know if I can . . . well, I am less and less sure that I am whom you take me for."
"Who else would you be?"
"Perhaps nobody."
"Strange idea."

"To me too. At the end of my road, I find myself, how shall I say, alone, without road."

"You have gone all the way."

"No doubt, but was it a way? You may think you are advancing and you are just marking time. Facing the abyss."

". . . or death."

"Death is not quite the same as the abyss. It is the infinite of a fascinating, but unlit place."

"And what is the abyss?"

"The obstacle, I am tempted to say. Whereas death is no obstacle, but a marginal springboard. We have to wait till we die to take wing. No road makes sense in death."

"And the empty page?"

"There are so many paths within the path."

"That's what you said—not in the same way, it is true—in *The Book of Questions.*"

"I hardly remember."

"You said: 'Where is the path? It must each time be discovered anew. A blank sheet is full of paths. And all these ways have their own ways. Else they would not be ways.

"'. . . Having our paths (or our possible paths) mapped out for us, why do we usually take the one which leads us away from our goal, leads us elsewhere, where we are not? But perhaps we are there also?'"

"I wrote those sentences in the Métro."

"You wrote them. They are yours."

"I remember . . . There was a man sitting near me at that time. A ridiculous man. Short and fat. His face puffy, red, hairy. His cap square in the middle of his skull. I wanted to laugh, but couldn't. I think I was listening for something which had trouble emerging, for which I had to look in myself, something both outside and inside, alien and intimate, as if deep down I had another self which refused my name and which I was condemned to bear, care for, to whose will I deferred in spite of myself, and which imposed its words. This has long puzzled me: I carry a stranger inside me whom I lavish my blood on, breathe my breath into, and know that he will remain a stranger. I cannot get rid of him.

"The man in the cap, the other riders, the car, the sequence of stations: this was my reality.

"If I were the author of the sentences you quoted, they would have closed in on this reality and worked it up. They would have been reflection and echo of what I saw, heard, or had saved up from other occasions. But, on the contrary, these sentences were intent on getting me out of my present, on abolishing everything around them in the name of a memory, a past, a life which had never been mine, but had become their own present, their ephemeral life. With its help they could finally die of my death."

"The words came to meet you to build the book with you."

"If you mean my works, you must know that they tolerated me only for as long as it took me to copy down their signs."

"You are in your books."

". . . as we are in the world, sure enough. But which fraction of sky or earth can we claim as ours?"

"The whole world."

"And emptiness?"

". . . that trap of time? . . . of a time dethroned for trying to lean on its own trap?"

"The time of the book."

> (*Hands reached out of the dark. Pudgy, heavy, long, bony, diaphanous hands. He saw them pass around the book, deck it with wings, catch it in mid-air, throw it in the fire, haul it out of the flames to bury it in the ground, and dig it up again to throw it into the water, as if it had to be at the heart of death and rebirth, the sacrificed, but always awaited word.*)

The Commentaries

1

"I am the interval."
"The interval is a hyphen."

2

It is well to compare ourselves to plants occasionally. What are they without their roots? For us, too, breaking our ties would mean ruin.

The world confirms that there is a soul living inside me.

The eye is double before the hand.

3

Make me a living torch to light up the night. Make me the eloquent life of fire. I am dead. All you can do is dust the earth with my ashes.

The living-dead. The living make excuses. The dead turn away.
The stone accuses.

Let granite be our Prince. Sand wins praise from
the sand.
The desert was our dice.

Ill-bred. Ill-starred. Ill-advised. Ill-used.
Ill wind fills our sails.

The love of centuries has gone towards the dark.

On the other side of the mirror, margins are
black.

4

The sky weeps only for the water.

"Soon the myriad pupils of the night," Sarah had
written, "will be one single eye.
"O Yukel, the sun is unity regained,
"all tears dried."

We are Jewish in our burning eyes.

5

"Is the question of the book a question of the
way?"
"The question comes always before the
question."

". . . our hands, Sarah, joined tenderly against
time, joined where there is no rest," wrote Yukel.

6

Yesterday, the void questioned your death, Sarah. Today, I question the void with you.

"Commentary," he said, "is the universe under-pinning the questions."
"We shall question the commentary."

One tear, and the eye is a question mark.

The First Evening on Ben-Yehouda Street in Jerusalem

"The book fidgets in its boundaries. Likewise, anxiety is at our borders," said Oury.

"Borders have always been our enemies," said Bethseba.

One city bears witness for all cities,
one grain of sand for the whole desert.

They had gathered in Oury's and Bethseba's small apartment on Ben-Yehouda Street.

Pinhas, Kadish, and Yonina were there. Pinhas said: "In *The Book of Questions*, you surround yourself with imaginary rabbis. True, what they say is very far from what most of our cantors of the Law deliver. But if you lent them your voice you must love them a little, must be grateful such persons exist. Yet you are not a practicing Jew. Or so you claim."

"For me," said Kadish, "God is without doubt the highest achievement of our prehistory, the writing before the writing you love. With God we attained our unity. But God lost the battle. Today, he looks like a tattered flag which no longer flutters in the wind. You seem haunted by this same image."

"I was struck, even moved," said Bethseba, "by the fact that the characters in *The Book of Questions* are each of their own time through what they say, no matter how modern their speech. Sometimes whole centuries of revolt and tears separate them, yet the same evil makes them contemporaries. For instance, when one of them notes: *A minute is enough to know a century*—one of the intentionally flat phrases which you liken, in "The Habit of Writing," to a pedestal—I hear it as if it came from the beginnings of the word. So I take its author to be the oldest of all in this immutable now which has been ours for centuries."

"If those irritatingly naïve sentences, which you present as *ramps of half-light*, show us where we are in the company of your characters," Pinhas continued, "they don't, for all that, tell us who we are. Are you Jewish? And what does being Jewish mean?"

"For me," said Oury, "the voice of your rabbis is your own. I too must ask you: Why rabbis?"

"When I was a little girl," said Yonina, "rabbis always seemed dark figures who had jumped out of the letters to make us read them. I suppose they embodied the mystery of the Book for me. Of prayers, I only listened to the songs. I've changed since. Yet at dusk, when my thoughts and eyes get lost on the horizon, the songs rise up again, and I cry."

"Yonina is marked by her Polish childhood," said Kadish. "Here, she has learned other songs. But to come back to your book: I think that your occasional use of rare, old-fashioned or forgotten words underlines the disturbance caused by fragmentation. You cannot get out except by a double inroad into the memory of the text. Before and after the usual word. Double break."

"Double destiny of word and man in the book," said Bethseba. "No word is ever altogether absent from any other. Writing unfolds around a scream. The real rabbis will never answer yours."

"You wrote, 'the sea never answers the sea,'" said Yonina.

"We have an answer to some of your questions," said Oury. "Will you accept it?"

"The answer is in the earth," said Kadish, "in our love of the earth."

"They say, the fruit is always the test of the question," replied Bethseba.

"Sour fruit," concluded Oury, "we'll reject you."

The Second Evening on Ben-Yehouda Street

This evening, Reuwen, Shimon, Yoshanan, and Uriel had come to see Oury and Bethseba.

Oury said: "*The Book of Questions* is from beginning to end interrupted in its unfolding. Each interruption is a cut. Gaping white wounds. Modesty of the page."

"Modesty of the word," continued Shimon. "The page is hunger."

"Thus the word is both desire and gift," said Uriel.

"*The Book of Questions*," said Yoshanan, "is the book of evening solitude, and inquiry is its star. The best morning takes place in the eyes."

"And the best death," added Reuwen.

"Death," said Bethseba, "is the sleep of the hours from which man does not awaken.

"Keep time awake, and you shall be eternal."

". . . like the earth," said Shimon.

"A thought for our dead," said Bethseba. "A thought for tears in the springtime of plants bathed in dew."

They fell silent. Then Reuwen said: "Did the sky not leave the sky for love of the earth? Did the sky not part with the earth for love of the sky?"

"The sky made the stone shiny and weightless in its passion for the beyond," said Bethseba.

(I do not know why I write or, rather, I know only too well.

If I keep writing in my night when I am nothing but invisible writing, if I cannot help writing, it is perhaps in order to resurrect in the eyes of another.

This hymn to completeness which, you said, has no home here, what is it but repressed desire turned into a song of the ardent desire of a book?)

Dialogue around Yaël and Elya

"Truth," he said, "is perhaps this worm which rues eating itself. O ruthlessness of God."

1

"There is no truth above man. There are only tenacious beliefs, the truths which consume us. The head is attacked first."

"Is emptiness the brow of a king?"

"The only truth is the truth of the crystal. Hard transparency of water."

"I do not believe in truth, but we must encourage each of its buds to open so that our true time may bloom in the sun. O promise of the lie."

"Truth, coveted virginity, vulnerable though hidden hymen. A few drops of blood after defloration reveal its sacrifice to the happy or cursed lover."

"Harsh approach, purity of the wound."

("Look," said Yaël, "look at this knothole in the branch, an eye gouged out by life, one of so many. Tell me, ah, tell me what merciful death will ever come to its aid?"

The sun has set. Tomorrow is the first day.)

2

(*"I love you,"* Yaël *had said,* "I love you. But all *your sperm could not drown three drops of my blood."*
"Lonely eye of the penis, swollen with lust:
"In the night of my flesh I have choked the genital whose spittle, for a brief moment of pleasure, spangled my dead womb with stars," said Yaël.)

"Is the book truth?"
"Truth is the key."
"Does the key adorn your belt?"
"I don't wear a belt."
"Does it adorn your neck?"
"I don't wear a necklace."
"Where is the key? Will we ever know?
"Nobody can read your book without it."
"On each of its pages, white flames melt the key."

(*"What I hold for true is what holds me for true.*
"O truth, how we dupe each other with clear heads," said Yaël.

We are inhabited by our metamorphoses.

Prophecy, the sin of survival.

The last song is the pariah's.)

3

He said: "our true face is the one we have in our hour of death, and death contrives to reduce it to dust."

Death has so often outstripped me in my books that we have become accomplices.

To catch the invisible in its fore-gestures and be led to the supreme gesture which kills us offhand.

What is written flows from a summary of life which the letters restore to its accepted boundaries. But farther off, out of reach, where life clings to its ruin and is nothing but a memory of man's predestined passage, there the universe finally lets us read it from the other side of memory. We alone, now, can do so.

Could God be the book? But in the book, God is without God as, in the word, man is without man.

God's silence has the dimensions of the Letter. In the abyss of the Name, God is the key to silence.

4

The invisible is a transparent circle of light, dark crowned by dark.

Time is naked.

Silence blurs the outlines of noise. Every sound is a star made dumb by distance.

We write while the words keep moving away.

> (*There is always a castaway who scratches his name on waves or sand with his nails. Life and death fight over it in every book.*)

5

Your sex, woman, is the empty eye of death.

"In suffering and in pleasure," said Yaël, "I have coldly watched you from my very soul and bruised entrails."

There is no secret for death.

Sun, target of hell,
dead eye covered
always, always
with arrows it spits at the day.
Only a fiery circle,
an eye burning in death
always, always.
Reflections, flames from beyond.

. . . only a circle which my feet unwittingly paced out in death.
Its center, the shameless iris.
    God's eye is everywhere.
    The void is a voyeur.

6

*("An eye for an eye,
the look insists."
"How come God refused to take this risk?")*

7

I have seen you laugh. I have seen you open the void with each guffaw.

Death is laughing. Sometimes I hear it, an echo of your laugh.

I tore up some of my pages in a rage.

How the void laughed at that.

It was in hysterics.

Hysterics.

On the last day, the world will be swallowed in a gratuitous laugh, in an eye.

>   (. . . *"A tooth for a tooth," that is why we say:*
> *"to devour with one's eyes."*
>
> *Elya, margin for two pairs of eyes.*)

The Crisis or the Three Phases of Waiting for Death

Hissing, stridulous breath. Soul and body only a
prolonged whistle. The world closing against itself.

He was lying down, reading a book he had just received. Then
gave up the book for the paper. It was midnight, perhaps a bit later.
He could not get to sleep. He breathed with difficulty. He half sat
up in bed, with the pillow propped against the wall. This position
seemed most comfortable. His stomach ached. Or was it his stomach? He felt as if a dam near his heart cut his breathing, and the pain
went as high as his gums. This he did not really mind much. What
was painful was not being able to breathe. He got up. Standing, he
thought, he would manage to breathe. The moment he went into
the bathroom he felt dizzy. He had barely time to grab the rounded
edges of the washbasin and leaned there with his forehead against
the mirror in front of him. He must not move, he thought, to help
the air pass through his chest. He was pale. He shivered. He waited
for the moment when his strength would give. Was there nothing to
help him this time? He had so much left to do. He must, above all,
be able to speak—but which revealing words would slit open his lips?
—to justify himself—but for what? Basically, his life had been a careful letting go. There was so much love which deserved, each time, a
new echo. At which page of the written book had he stopped? And
why this page rather than another? At which page of the book he
was writing would he stop? Was it words smothering him? Was it
the book with every one of its frustrated words?

(My own enemy. Without resources. I am not drawn towards day, but, on the contrary, towards an ancient night which has, paradoxically, become my hermitage. Dispossessed, I seem to have a name for the first time.

My body is wasting away so fast you can see it. Power of a breath of air. Could God be the Breath of breaths?)

The needle of a syringe in the most visible vein of his right arm made him jump. So he was not alone. Somebody—his doctor, no doubt—said: "The heart is not in danger." And: "There must be a cause for this attack, a psychological cause." There would be many loops to be looped. But where to start? He remembered nothing of the immediate past. He hovered between life and death. Now he was cold as on a winter night, now he perspired. Was he living whole seasons in a second? Everything around him accelerated its pace. In our last moments, we take giant steps, but going where? He was still standing, incapable of the smallest movement.

(I fight, unable to bear it, legs and fists tied, against an undefinable evil.

Who have I been? Often I would not show my face: for which other self might I have been taken? It was my own fault I no longer had either name or country. I tried to reassure myself that I was Everything. In my moments of depression, I admitted I was Nothing, and my signature at the bottom of my stationery, where the words of my joys and sufferings were lined up, put together two syllables nobody could read. But to whom was I writing anyway?

*In this signature of mine I saw the random de-
sign of a destiny without attachments, the progres-
sive blotting out of distant reality.*

*I wrote to Yaël. I had never interrupted the corre-
spondence with my dead love. Large empty sheets
brought her replies.)*

He was dripping. It seemed his brain was no longer irrigated by
his blood, but by some kind of, probably yellow, liquid: sweat or
urine? Malodorous gift from his feverish body. His head stank. For
how many hours is a dead man in control of his thoughts? And how
many days do his thoughts resist the onslaught of the void?

O time of uncertain absence of time. Unable to assert anything,
yet daring to suppose all.

He no longer had a mouth, just a useless cavity where air was re-
luctant to venture. Voices droned in his ears and spread in a confused blur.

*(I remember I reacted with amusement when a
friend told me that during my recent absence from
Paris, the papers had reported my death.*

*I did not feel concerned. I had often joked about
the futility of a life so fragile that it could be broken by a mere nothing. Wrongly, by the way. Did I
not know that the very precariousness of my life
was the condition of my enlisting in tow of a truth I
would never catch up with, a truth which only the
void holds? Any weakness is a frontier crossed toward death.*

. . . Any weakness, a heaven-sent door.

*Does the mind, at the end, take possession of the
body?*

*Does the mind, in death, take on all the weight
of the body?*

Even beyond, where the flesh is no more,
the word is carnal.

The void is the definitive desertion of the body.
The mind abdicates.

The void acquires a presence which the absence
of the universe has to concede.
However, this void is not the truth—it cannot
have any direct relation to truth. But it is the door
through which we enter truth and walk among its
benign or malign tumors towards oblivion where
our unions were sealed.)

There was much pressure from the outside, urgent and strong. He had to resume his life in a burst of solidarity with the present in order to recover, through old ties and derelictions, his face so often spurned.

If the end was gradually revealed to him, the morning after the end remained a mystery. Deciphering it, of course, carried its own end within itself.

Fine sand. Final sand. Thoughts get bogged down here.

Was he nothing but a thought at the bottom of the hierarchy?

Had he not gone from estate to estate with a Sovereign's crown on his head, exploring his kingdom? But tonight the whole earth had him by the throat. Flayed, on a path bordered with thorns, he would soon be only the awkward tracing of a thousand mortal wounds.

His doctor's phrase circled in his head like a moth round a lamp. The whirring of wings, which so irritated him, seemed to come from another world. There are hunks of sky knocked about by the wind. We will never know their story though they cling to our memories of the dead.

(*O sun, fiercy circle disavowing the circle.*

Does the center then deny the center, the precise point challenged by the curve which doubt has stopped in mid-soar?

Nothing but longing for the well we can no longer imagine?)

WANDERING

"The book is my home. It has always been the home of my words."

"You lived by words which were stolen again and again. My words are this home."

"Then I won't have any words?"

"Then I won't have any home?"

First Approach to the Book
(The Blank Page)

He said: "I am wandering, the wandering of all wanderings, the one and only wandering: alone."

"This absence which claims the book in order to rewrite it, is this God and, therefore, the hope for a divine word which devours us?" he asked.

The name of God holds the word in check.

In the word, God declares a check on God.

THE FACE

Where is your face?
You have none. Perhaps
you are not human.
I shall give faces to those like me
so they can talk and laugh.
I shall triumph over the face.
Yet did not God say: "Thou shalt not kill"?

God's face is smoother
than an infant's forehead.
It is your womb, woman,
that gives shape.
And the nurse:

It is my breasts, woman,
that give shape.
And the stranger:
It is death, woman,
that gives shape.

THE BURDEN

Anguish at the flight of hours, not because I fear death, but because it is impossible to live, impossible to follow.
Between two banks, my love, the river is the burden.

THE BODY

I carry my days and proud nights where I forgive
your body for taking away my world.

The body is close, the soul distant. Thus we are both absent and present.
Absent from where we think we are, present where we are not.
The body can be touched. It is what is touched, caressed, stroked—and what touches, caresses, strokes and strokes itself.
The soul is the life within the body, the body is the soul in mourning.
The soul comes before, the body after.
Before, there is the infinite, after, the finite.
What is finished is forever borne by the soul.
The unfinished ravages the body, immolates your face to time.
Your face has your age. Face of all times within time, both unfaithful and the same.
We are outstripped.

(*The body
peoples forth*.)

THE INVISIBLE

The infinite cleaves us, and we are an everlasting scream.

What is visible is fraud.
The invisible impugns it.

Complexity is a game of the visible to attract the invisible.

God is invisible. I have often seen Him such as He could appear to me. All appearance manifests something invisible at the edge of horizons, which we seize by its legitimate desire to be. Can the traces of eternity—the unending part of something at its end—be measured by the size of the wound that matter exhibits, as by the banished star's repeated and vain recourse to the light which for a moment dazzled it? The sky is flecked with so many neuralgic points—each the culmination of a fall—that nobody could make them out. Matter is a crossroads, drawn and quartered. But the route beyond becomes less and less passable, the dots of its line farther and farther apart until nothing distinguishes it from the void.

(*Deciphering of absence, gauge of the No.*)

Time affirms, confirms what is; eternity denies.
God is in time, not in eternity.
Thus God has killed God.

(*Words take our sight away so as to be the only ones that see. They will be our pupils.*)

The All shows itself in the book. It condemns us, after a cruel selection process, to die, in despair, of ourselves.

Having seen all means also having effaced all.

Writing injures our retina more seriously each time.

On every page of the book, our eyes are stuck.

From the other side of death, the desert stares at us with our own eyes.

> *(For silence, the image speaks. For the word, the invisible is the silence where God defines himself.*
>
> *To learn to see where there is no more world.*
>
> *The letter is the last figure of absence. In death, the book gives itself to the book.)*

Man is light. God is behind man.

Let my light never become walled-in eyes. The road anticipates the road.

To make an inventory of the thousand and more nights within one night. The first evening of the fore-world sparkled with *incipit*.

> *(To reach, by stages, the invisible at the end of what we have, in the course of our life, cast off as ballast to oblivion. To enter eternity, the ultimate quenched look, the last lamp burned out.*
>
> *Night is an endless abode. In vain, we tried to live in bright daylight, afraid of the dark.*
>
> *God burned for God.)*

Rims of foam on the beach: does the universe end here?

All birth is blank like death.

We have followed the intractable course of the water upstream.

What is done is as soon undone.

Already, tomorrow is just a hand lost to the hand.

The soul is a halfway house of eternity. The body gives in to the body until thirst makes it transparent.

God is the mirror of a distance in tune with its reflections.

The abyss has been looked at.

> (*When adventure has reached its farthest point where the sea listens only to the sea, writing suddenly appears as a broken coastline which no map records.*
>
> *But which good fairy's punctual fingers light up house after house at night?*
>
> *He who is written questions in his exile the page which accepts him.*
>
> *The void recognizes the word.*)

Second Approach to the Book
(The Tie)

1

A look is not knowledge, but a door.
Seeing means opening doors.

"Is all this mine?" he asked.
He was answered: "Does the desert belong to
the grain of sand, or the sky to the highest cloud?"

How can we understand God outside writing?
What will be written is what He has pronounced.

Discipline of being, spiritual rule of life. I try to
hear you, and already your words exist only in my
diligent zeal to listen.

"Save the cloud," cried the storm.

2

Creating your truth means exalting the instant. I salute eternity
from one second to the next. The rope falls in love with the fingers
that braid it. It is not truth which triumphs, but the creature in
bondage, man, the days, the captive lungs.

I went out into the street. It was not the street, but the rainbow after the shower, which joins the world of the day to the end of the world.

I had only my eyes to help me get used to life.

Passing, among things passing.

For generations of lovers obsessed with the universe there will be left stones and what little is known of what has been.

There will also be left words of passion, long gagged, but which the lips, garrulous and crafty receivers, will bring to light.

The violators of graves are legion.

Wherever you go there is water, earth, sky. Wherever you are warm there is fire. Wherever you try to advance there is wind. Wherever you lie down to sleep there is the cold without make-up. There are, above our numb limbs, maternal nights to cradle the ocean of scuttled worlds.

A highway is also a humble crossroad, and most often we do not know where it leads.

Worlds are stirring here, and we die of their blindness.

Freedom, whose wings have taken all the credit, has recourse to the abyss to cement its foundations.

The trunk goes about rising, the fruit ripens at the heart of its checked flight.

Third Approach to the Book
(Answer to a Letter)

> God is born of His immortal desire to die of
> God.

You ask me many questions. I cannot really answer them all, but will try to get at some in a roundabout way. This questioning will take me over certain obscure routes which I followed alone and which abandoned me at dawn, at the parting of my ways. As if departure came after the journey. As if we forever prepared to leave, knowing we could reach only the excruciating point of departure.

Any advance is terror and trial of the first step. So with each letter in the word, with each word in the sentence, the Book begins.

Intimate ways, therefore, which I could not exhaust except inside myself. Ways leading me to the brink of being where all presence surrenders to thirst: a quest of poverty, I would say, in a labyrinth like those of glass at fairs, which draw crowds that gather, amused, watching, pointing their fingers at you. A labyrinth where you are seen, but do not see. Sure, after much groping, the exit will be found. But it has given us only the measure of the maze. How many others are there that we never get out of?

Contrary to what you seem to think, I find it very difficult to write. When I take my pen all doors close in front of me. The country, the world folds shut. In this closed universe, every word—even while I form it—becomes a lock in which I turn the key. Imprisoned, I no longer know where to knock.

I have entered each of my books with the very clear impression that I was not expected or, rather, that I had been expected for so long that it finally despaired of my coming. As if the book belonged only to the words, and they were—or were no longer—ready to let themselves in for an adventure I could not help proposing. Hence these inevitable moments of uncertainty, of hesitating at the threshold of the work, which constantly require proof that the quest is important—when it is perhaps illusory in its essence. A quest whose merits the author must affirm in spite of misgivings and distress. In fact, it is much more a matter of sizing up risks than of trying to snare the words in traps into which the author would fall first. To go toward death, to make a death for himself as you would make a life, this is, I think, his task in the book. He will, then, identify with the words after measuring himself against them. In a universe filled with syllables, he will assume a manifold name, having learned that every letter is a name. When the initiative escapes him, when his voice suddenly stops taking the lead, he knows he is finally writing, has been written, and represents from now on a tiny part of the book which is surging forward and will destroy him as it breaks. Drowned where the ocean roars, he will, for a moment of eternity, lift his head. But only in passing, to salute the sky which no passion and no suffering can wrinkle.

The book is engulfed by the book. But the word is innocent wherever it gives in to the urgent promptings of an unknown force, a voice more sonorous than its own, augural absence of a voice which fascinates and makes it tremble. Death in its prime gets drunk on the screams of our own deaths. We rise and founder out of the same shared daring.

Before the book which we are closing in on, dozens of books blossom and die without us, in a forgotten space hardly touched by words. Hence every word, beside its own life woven of many lived lives which remain unknown—every word, in responding to our entreaties, eludes innumerable existences which we have dreamed or imagined, and of which we let it catch a glimpse: possibilities it could have had. You must not think words are without memory. Where we have erased everything, they are present to remind us in a stroke of lightning, a singular light, of our past, of what it could have been and what it was.

Before the book, then, where we struggle without memories, elusive moments of the book inscribe themselves into its plan and expectation. So that you never know but what the book is already in this fore-book full of questions asked only of the book, and which it tries to answer as if independent.

Between our questions and those the book asks on its own, the work is done and undone with our help. Facing the task, we are listening to a truth which never surrenders except in its winding paths and humiliating returns to an emptiness which only the ocean can fill. The book's truth is that fraction of time when it breaks from its totality to meet the page, the phrase, the symbol, which it has made bleed from the start.

Ah, do we know how much, while we pursue it, we are without idea, without need, without image?

Innate innocence of the verb matching the naïveté of a crowd which hope or despair draws to a fixed place where their future is at stake. The verb displays its innocence up to the moment of dizziness when it claims to possess the truth.

Does original sin perhaps persist within a truth we glory in championing? On those who claim to own it truth takes ruthless revenge. How many of our fellows have died of its spears. How many works it has quashed with the proper weapon.

Truth impossible to pass on, a sister of silence and the abyss. Is the white page perhaps its preferred repository? All whiteness is violence, like the wall's mute determination to block our road. All whiteness is God's color, which in the silence of an infinite truth pierces our eyes and crushes. Is the writer's struggle not this mad effort to sink his hands into the sand of the shore just once before the wave takes him back? White page, tormented, strong in its will from beyond the sea whose wave, raging to devour the port, hollows out the bottom with unwearying effort. God is in the wall. God is in the wave. Our arms, our moans will henceforth only try to mitigate His violence until forced to give in.

The convict in his tower will end up screaming to escape the cruelest punishment: smothering in the word, in the absence of words. Likewise the writer, and also the word, both always at a distance from their short lives. There is no jailer, no reader so inattentive that he has not heard their pathetic appeals to life.

Screams that have turned into sheaves, into dawn. Strange lands whose survival we have hailed, dead voices which show the way within the way and which you can no longer ignore. Hard stages before the promised peace.

Is writing simply to rise up against silence, a twitch of life within death, and finally to die of its passion? Die with its passion whose death catches us unawares with its loss of energy like a setting sun? O night, vast tomb of oblivion. And it is no common coincidence if we can see our suppressed words shining in the dark like epitaphs frozen in their eternal order. But will we be granted a total, inviolable peace? The dream betrays the violence of silence. And the unconscious, which troubles and disturbs us, is finally nothing but a silenced word. Could there be an end which is sleep without haunting dreams or shores? Certainly not in the book.

Around what is not expressed, what we could never formulate, we talk like the deaf and write blindly, outside time. But life is there, on our heels, life come to meet us where we stoically tried to do without it. What does it want from us? And first of all, what hold does it have on the book? O weight of the prelude. All steps are under its sign. But life carries death in its womb, and we have eaten of this death.

Silence, where the word abdicates, is also the exemplary death of God. Our tears and every dry root in the desert bear witness to it.

Is speaking then the attempt to fill the void left by the death of God? One speaks to God as one speaks to the far side of silence, that is to say, to the shadow of a shadow which will brighten and then cast us out.

Will you accuse me of being a writer of death? You reproach me for effacing myself in the name of the book. as if the writer could not but proclaim, once he is aware of it, that he cannot possibly exist? "Unable to be who I am, let the book henceforward be. In it, I have my chance to endure." He cannot possibly exist (though as an individual he may) as a "partaker" in the burning of an instant tuned to his defeat, as a "participant" in the birth of a star whose dark spots we will later start to count. Nothing in the man who grapples with the white page catches our attention. He may be powerful or poor, engaging or ugly, gentle or a tyrant, he is what he becomes, and what he becomes does not recognize him. And yet this creature of absence lives; and his life is a sketch of mysteries. In bending over it he loses his reality. Thus he loses his name by the very naming.

Is speaking, at this point, perhaps pledging your being to a series of metamorphoses across a space affected by the hour, but where time is powerless? Could it further mean silencing within the word all toying with allegiance to the universe where it is watched over at the limits of its space and carried like a bird into the flowering infinite?

And does the word perhaps, in its last flight, become visible and invent a script both secret and monumental which we will claim as our own for having watched from the ground how it grew?

But are we, in the long run, implicated? To answer yes would mean holding ourselves responsible for the steep of the cliff or the impetuous heave of the wave. Is it not, however, through us that ocean and cliff define themselves, through us that they communicate?

All-linking hyphen, the writer wishes to be an unbreakable bond in order to regain his footing. His bond is a noose across the abyss where the word escapes and leaves him hostage. A circle at first, then the writer less and less at ease in this circle until he can no longer move. Come morning, the knot gives, and he's in the void again, bruised to his very soul by a truth whose face he has lost.

Burnt out millions of years ago, certain stars continue to shine for us. Absence lures us beyond death which is the formal access to absence.

Is writing simply the way in which that which expresses itself without us nevertheless expresses itself through what has been handed down to us from our origins and which the word made us discover?

I have eyes only for what I do not see and what, I know, will soon dazzle me. The road stretches between its two beginnings. The sun burns in the night instead of pulsing, or perhaps pulses while burning, certainly remains a pulse. Death is an accomplice of creation. Death is the absent place where the book waits for its fulfilment.

Fourth Approach to the Book
(On the Nature of Obstacles)

You show yourself only to hide what you are, O void, O nothing. What is not wants to be free to be. And this freedom becomes the obstacle you run up against.

The space between words could be considered the moment when the word falls silent in order to cross the distance which separates it from itself. But this distance is immeasurable.
O premature death.
White space, foam of the shipwreck, eternal hymn to the drowned.

O blank, unnamed page, you put a yeasty truth in our hands.
Did we know that this truth was no other than yourself?

He said: "Like the words, we can only live on the white surface of the page.
"The obstacle is inside."

The void bears the weight of the universe, though light as air.

All truth is airy.

". . . The obstacle," I replied, "is the whiteness.
We write on it in the hope of getting around it."

In the word *vivre*, "to live," there is the word
ivre, "drunk."

"You steeve the cargo of a ship," he said, "but
ah, what counterweight of silence will balance the
part of my life converted to words?"

Giddy with space, the wind ends by dropping
away pitifully.

Muzzle the waves. The dogs will stop barking.
Becalmed. Becalmed.
Clear sky is a deathbed.

Clear face of God.
What transparency in faith!

The obstacle is what does not immediately present itself as an
obstacle.
The obstacle is precisely the absence of obstacles.
The outer wall of the Temple in Jerusalem is an example: its every
stone is a springboard for prayer. Outside, emptiness blocks not
only the passage of bodies, but also the outpourings of the soul, the
entreaties, praises, screams. Stone helps the take-off, space breaks
it. God enters into our words to stop being an obstacle. He dies with
them. The death of God is a broken barrier.
The milestones on the road sing freedom, but also tell its failure.
Our lives end at the foot of a wall, the ultimate wall, which is
invisible.
The void is the oldest pitfall.

(*Writing is born with death, yet is life in progress.*

The origins of life are spread over the void in stages listening for a chance to rise into the world of the instinctive word. To learn its name. The book is joined in the book.

Tomorrow you will read yourself where you almost died a hundred times.

You do not know who you are. You will know who you are becoming.

Death is the cruel soul of life. Spirit of flame and night. The body is the fruit of its strength.)

Fifth Approach to the Book
(Y.H.W.H. or the Unpronounceable Name)

1

(I am speaking of the Jew. I say: JEW, but I am thinking mostly of the word itself, any word, the letter, the last sign which is a point—the center of Nothing, drenched with ink and blood—which holds up the book and all its weight of light and night: a minuscule star, a yellow star. And is not the most striking representation of the infinite the three points of the ellipsis, three tiny yellow stars?

I repeat: The sign is Jewish.

The word is Jewish.

The book is Jewish.

The book is made of Jews.

Because the Jew has for centuries wanted to be a sign, a word, a book. His writing is wandering, suspicion, waiting, confluence, wound, exodus, and exile, exile, exile.)

2

He said: "The name of God is the consummate name. The letters which disclose it would indicate its limits if such were conceivable."

3

Abolishing His Name, God broke all His ties because He knew that every name is an indestructible knot.

There is a law which governs the absence of the book. It is the law which the book announces and to which it refers in order to be a book.

Law within the revealed Law. We read it in the margins.

4

Judaism is always outside Judaism. It is a religion of leaving the word behind in its own absence and austere novelty, where the face anxiously waits for the face.

The desert knows the weakness of such names.

5

You are opened by your eyes.

The book tells the era of an ancient seed and separation, those of the fruit within the seed.

The universe is scored with claims, and their echo reverberates in the birth of a word. Hence writing consists first in answering unknown voices, in spying continually on a voice whose barren efforts perforate time from the inside.

PARALLEL EXISTENCE I

No doubt you think I am wrong. But have I not since childhood been the innocent prey of my contradictions?

You ask about my origins. I reply that they are in the book. Not where God asserts Himself, but where he withdraws into a Word struck deaf and blind.

I like God blind and deaf so I can forgive him those two terrible senses, hearing and sight. We alone will see, will hear for God.

Is it possible that original sin is first a sin of the Creator? Otherwise, where is the origin? Could God have deceived God?

Tragical dispute of a conscience elevated into an example, but which knows that the road to purity goes through the sin it condemns.

The unconscious part of creating is the divine part. We are bound to God beyond all knowledge, beyond Good and Evil, that is, beyond the unquestionable gesture of the Creator.

Are the conscious beings sacrificed to the universe? Can the marvelous unity in the word only be accomplished with our last gasp?

And then nothing, nothing but the fullness of an instant no longer ours.

Do we have to be defeated to write? Is writing itself the force which strikes us down? I have learned to crawl. But who will help me in my exile? My hand, cut off from the world, drifts in my blood.

"Be saints because I am," said Yahweh. That is to say: For love of Me become Me in sainthood. And did He not also say: "Be different from other peoples as I am different from other gods?"

Thus, through God, through His asserting Himself as an only God, sainthood and separation, sainthood and otherness have become synonyms.

The saint as well as the writer is separate in God's image: separate in the gap between the appointed—or reappointed—signs, dark space punctuated here and there by the stars of passion and death. We can conceive of the infinite by the distance of its landmarks which confine us. Tomorrow approaches from the farthest of days after, where our oldest past slumbers.

Is the writer different by his wish to perpetrate the saintly task of recognizing the voice of God, though long dead, in his own—as if he had died with God in order to hear His voice and then to disappear in his own time?

Because it is definitely against the silence of God and man, against the residual magnetism of this silence, that the word revolts. Towards this silence, subsoil of all interrupted silence, the writer is gradually driven. In it, the word dies.

Does writing then mean perishing of a word as inseparable from others as a grain of sand, which death consecrates by singling it out?

Death is holy as the forbidden name of God is holy. To stand aside, to be your own avoidable effacement, holding a word which no page can formulate or contain, but on which bursts a cloud of words which delivers us to its secret by annihilating us.

". . . Gliding silence which jostles its own silence," he said.

Water which has circled the letter, which the Jew stoops to drink, but which, like the water of the Sacred Texts, never quenches your thirst. Prodigal water whose flow unrolls like an echo the stanzas of faultless love which fill its soul.

In back of this water, of this indefinitely repeated song, the journey begins. Page after page. In back of this water where the desert stretches, there is set down the long march of a hopeless people led by hope. Because this is their strangeness: that they are the most pessimistic people and at the same time heartened by an irreducible hope.

I who do not believe or, rather, whose faith is an endless virgin night, I have never felt more strongly that I belong to this people of the Book than in the desert, between All and Nothing, in this Nothing which little by little appropriates All by eroding it. There our routes start which have no goal, but nevertheless let us arrive. Endless routes whose every halt, every pause imposed by fatigue or discouragement, is a milestone on the combined paths of ancestral wisdom. Milestones which later change into books, books which are exchanged for every meditated page of the book.

The man born of the milestone is read in what will be written tomorrow and what the words express already, as if everything had been said once and had taken possession of the vast world, englobing past and future, as if our time to live only existed in abolished time, in the very abolishing which gives it a dimension beyond measure.

What begins by dying or, more exactly, what calls for breath in order to live its death, grows and dies in solemn repetition of God's advent in the heart of the creature condemned to renew its pact with death until the fatal surrender.

Subtle relation of man to the time of the book which is not, as we now know, the time of the word, but the time which precedes and outdistances the word, time where the letter burns in its own fire and avowal. Time of manure and ashes. Ears of grain make the beauty of fields and feed man, but the scream and the wound of all birth belong to the void, to the triumph and spectacular fall into emptiness where the universe questions its luminous fragments left after its sudden explosion from within. Fall which comes after the presumptuous triumph of any presence in the world, fall described by the diffuse intensity of every ray of the star sought by the dark and the hour. Fall of day and starry night, which do not question the existence of the star, but our ability to catch it. Out of sight, in its turbid will to live or in the retreat of a night, everything pursues its particular life. The dark taught us this long before the light. Thus death appears in our image as a dramatic episode: a presence perceived, then lost to our senses, its rise and decline.

Drama of man's separation from the universe which takes place in eyes giddy with seeing, a soul in love with unity. We shall never embrace the infinite, yet it is our dream, our concomitant reality.

Eternity speaks to us, and we burn with ignorance. Knowledge is a bubble which bursts in the least breath of air. In refusing images, the Jew refuses himself. But this refusal springs from the desire to go all the way in the fever which discolors the image till it becomes its own desperate emancipation.

Chance of the desert: the ear warns the eye of the stealthiest approach. The sand disputes the existence of God.

A book persists in the same way as a thought devoted to writing.

God is the source of what is written. Thought which recognizes the primacy of the Letter, which makes it the basis of His contemporaneousness. Does the Temple represent the upright Letter? The Temple was built in the book. God renounced the body for the book with every letter.

In parallel to deciphering, before any book, an existence trammeled between God's gesture and man's in the free space where creature fuses with creation, the Jews dispersed over the five continents, where their fate is shunted onto the margins, learn to reconcile their vocabulary with their oldest memory. It too a sign within the sign, it weighs on the word and charges it with all the unexplored paths of the book. Paths of the One toward the One, as if the innumerable gathered in the unique to form the straight line which our rereading of the world and its beings would break and again mend. Line claiming to be proof of the permanence—across two languages, one of them dead—of a race which death and life fashioned from one single word

. . . from one identical word learned or unlearned according to the day. Oblivion, glacial, intermediate zone, unites people and planets in the implacable hour when it comes due. To pay our tribute to the void. To backtrack. God is always *between*, superbly oblivious of time,

forever oblivious of man and time, which is why the creature revolts.

Against oblivion. All prayer is leavened by remorse of existing without God. Man falls in love with his singing and turns it into a hymn to the glory of Creation. In truth, he speaks to his own absence. Absence defined by the universe.

Against divine oblivion, but not against God. The prophet's voice forgives, though bent by stones. Voice of silence with the letter as seal.

Silence is the doorway of oblivion. Man approaches his end from silence to silence.

"Writing of silence, letters of chalk," he said.

The faith which rules the believer tends to give memory back to God. If you get God to remember, does this mean that in finding a susceptible memory buried in universal memory you depend on nothing else for writing God?

By death's side we go through barren and hidden fields.

Man and God face their mutual recollections. As they are written. As man relives them from book to book.

Does dying mean going to the far end of memory in death? Could there be a posthumous effort of memory to appropriate the memory of God?

Man gets tarnished in death as God does from image to image.

"Stop offending our eyes with these painful yellowed pictures of yourselves," he said. "Quick, let's get to the last one which retains only the vaguest memory of an image."

Existing means holding on to the day. Dying means emptying the dark of any reminiscence of light. It means, step by step, entering total night.

God, death and man reach eternity together, which is another form of oblivion.

(*Scruple of the believers to whom falls the privilege of resuscitating God in each of their acts, each of their thoughts. A rule with a care for life, this rule inspired by divine procedure, that is to say, a rule which turns man into the attentive reader of a universe whose truth plants flowers along the way in order to compel recognition with the faded petal. Twilight apotheosis.*

Thus joy and distress are alternating stanzas of one and the same prophetic song.)

Keeping the faith with God means keeping it with man in his quest for truth. Tracks within the hollow of the Track. Stimulating differences. God is the sum of our differences.

Respect for the law is, first of all, respect for man in his diverse ways of facing his individuality, which is made more difficult by the gesture placing it opposite his responsibilities. To be in the truth, to reach it with our feeble means. Written law is utterance joined with its end. Afterwards, there is nothing. There is the self-sufficiency of a world which rejects the word, the immense available space of accrescent writing watched over by centuries of nocturnal writing.

(With each breath the flame of the candle wavers and becomes one of our twenty-two exhumed letters. It derives its light from death.
Seven-armed candelabrum, seven times death celebrates our survival in death.)

Reading the law is reading yourself. But which reading of yourself across God could be unique? We read the same words, and their sense divides us in order to unite us in solitude. There they leave us.

God is alone with man where man is without God.

(. . . without God, that is, before God, before man, in the unmarred dark where the book lights up.)

. . . God, Totality in process, foreseeable only for Him.

Reading the Law is reading death.

PARALLEL EXISTENCE II

Our wandering around the world could only be
the long circling of a word.
Word like a wager in the name of man and at the
mercy of the emptiness where it moves.

Imagine a tree which no longer puts forth leaves, a soil no longer
like soil, an insistent sob through the ages. And in this sob, penciled
in as it were, innumerable faces with mine among them.

*(Being Jewish does not mean being born of a dif-
ference, but of a separation deepened by centuries.*

*Always evicted, left stranded in his suffering as
on the tracks of the next best station—or pushed
into the first train to depart—the Jew keeps his
eyes on the horizon. We will remember the unset-
tling image of his face taking on farewell features
which distance will gradually wear away.*

*"Over there we'll be together. You and me. Over
there we'll have a home and be happy."*

*Elsewhere. Here. Why not here? Here, a re-
discovered elsewhere.*

*Being Jewish means having vainly tried to put an
end to separation by adapting to a likeness we
hoped everyone would recognize.*

*Are we forgetting that, struck in his origins, the
Jew bears the wound of hostile gestures, of words
of storm and lightning hurled against him?*

*Excluded. Naked. Naked like the destroyed Tem-
ple, the witness wall.*

*In his wound and his words, which are born of
both the Word of truth and the hostile words of
men, protected by the Book and delivered up to his*

*enemies in power, the Jew anxiously turns his fate
into an intransigent exploration across death which
he inaugurates and is prepared to obey.*

*Dead of wanting to live against life, alive by vir-
tue of being lost in death's labyrinth, he comes into
his own in survival, as if the beyond were his place.
So his words remain prophetic and announce the
return of those who left the time of man.*

*Time of brotherhood predicted by the victim of
an inhuman time—tomorrow always means the
approach of hope—time of the earth.*

*The peculiar nature, the strangeness of the Jew:
these are in his second face carved by obsession, by
his neighbors' imagination, second face which takes
the place of his own when people scrutinize him.
Excessive features. Caricature or faulty sketch? If
they exist, the peculiar nature, the strangeness of
the Jew can only reside in a non-face, a subjective
negative. Negative of a space within the space to be
filled, engraved, and then denounced, space whose
features they show and which, on the other hand,
is the link that makes the Jew recognize his Jewishness outside himself—as if you could be yoked to
others by a chain of openings onto the infinite
Nothing.*

*Thus the Jew lives in the lie of others. He invents
himself inside the invention of others. Stepping out
of himself he does not see himself as they see him,
but as he knows he can never be seen.*

*"Search my soul," he seems to ask. But what for?
The soul does not lie. Perhaps to escape finally the
lies and his own parody.*

*Being Jewish means therefore being at the heart
of an essential interrogation. Called into question
by the heirs of his questions, his certainties glow*

under the ashes. For every day is a day of ordeals.
Stirring the ashes, how many hours do we awaken
that were never seized?

He might well have discovered through mere
personal experience that the earth is round. His
speech is circular and self-sufficient. The universe
inside the circle.

His inner life is the deeper for his not having any
other, as it were.

Even more than by his speech the Jew is a Jew by
the silence or the vast murmur which encloses his
eyes as a sea surrounds an island and makes it
inaccessible.

For the Jew, the world must be read from the
middle of the main, in the calm or booming of
waves. The vastness of silence can be as shattering
as an exploding shell.

The Jewish soul, always on the alert, knows the
torment of water ploughed and whipped by the
wind. Lightning is thought to be God's threatening
finger. A fraction of a second will do to reduce
time, our time, to dust.

This frightening, crushing silence which in its
finest moment, when God called on His people, di-
vided and split in order to speak to itself, split into
divine silence and the silence of the creature: this
silence is what the broken Tables of the Law give us
to meditate. Double silence which the inscribed
stone perpetuates in a second birth. Silence of the
word and silence of the outlived moment closed
forever on its own hunger.

God's language—language of absence, language
of a language that has weathered fire and marble
frost—is unalterable, as if spelled by death. Com-
posed of eternal signs it refuses the life of whatever
accent.

Thus, because it cannot be heard, the name of
God wants to be unpronounceable and sterilize the
letter at the height of its meaning.)

PARALLEL EXISTENCE III

I am a plant in action, he said.
And I a plant in agony, the other replied.
And added: Finally I am a place. Ah, that you
would tell the world.

. . . But what is then the virtue of the sacred Book, of the Book of
Books? Could it be example rather than lesson? The lesson of the
example? Model of all books, it is immortal for being copied.

Looking toward the Book, solitary with his fellows who, like him,
are eager readers of their history, the Jew declares himself a Jew
through his ties, accepting their claims.

Mad pride to think you are yourself, when nobody can help being
another.

Do we have nothing in common but the road?

. . . We have nothing in common and at the same time everything: an unshakable faith in the book. But for you, the book is a
place of refuge, for me, a link with exile, with death, that is, a link
with a word which for dying of its merits deprives us of our place,
link with the sacrifice to a word to which we cannot come back and
which is closed against our fervor.

Exile within the essence of ties, part of the very nature of ties.
Exile conjoined with exile.

Tie to a fierce and naked word whose place is the center of a
ruined world, the middle of a sunk universe.

Desert. All writing is first of all a wound of sand. Thus the He-
brew people had to spend forty years in Sinai in order to identify
with the Book.

The desert wrote the Jew, and the Jew reads himself in the desert.

Cries in the constancy of the sign and, in these cries, songs of victory and subjection. Burst of rootless words which the Jew tried to plant in his soul and which have blossomed in his mouth.

Is the serpent sentenced to letting us read God in its slither?

"My hand sees with eyes of its own. My pen is its tongue. The head of a reptile takes shape on my paper," he said.

"The mouth," he added, "is the promised land. Every word we speak means we return to the land,

"means we enter through words into an exiled Word buried in the sand."

The desert is the distance of our destiny. In this distance, our voices run dry.

Man spoke after God, but God had spoken for man. Thus one and the same word is our common origin. With every word, we are by God's side, at the threshold where the initial silence begins to be heard.

"Owning land means owning a word."

"The loved word recurs often in the book."

"Land of your own is more than syllables in harmony. It is a collective dream, a vow to live."

"Within man, the world is a heap of reclaimed words."

"And the book? An offering of sheets among books?"

"Writing a destiny, design of a word."

("*The people chosen by God,*" *he said,* "*had to be excluded as God was by His Name.*

"*In this exclusion lies our identity. Any reading of our particularity is a poignant reading of our strangeness.*"

And he added: "*For consolation, I sometimes indulge in thinking that it is for the book we have suffered so much.*"

*Could one man meet another if they were not
both in the book?*

*Do we use a planetary language to address God
as if He had left us a taste for a universal word toward which our words converge,*

for a word both dawn and dusk?

Does God confuse our voices?

*"Any word of love," he said, "has one direction
only. Unanimous word."*

*Lost in the desert, he howled: "Now I know. Wa-
ter comes after death.")*

"Show us an image of exile," he was asked.
He drew an island. And explained:
"The word is an island.
"The book is an ocean peopled with islands.
"The book is a sky with scatterd stars.
"Island and star are figures of exile.
"Ocean and sky are exile within exile
"and law of exile.
"Exile is in the law, because the law
"is a book
"within the word."

No wall can mask a flustered truth surprised in its dawn nudity.

*(The commentaries on the Law are salutary
steps in the Word of the Creator defeated by Himself, Word where the spirit blows beyond recall.*

*Thus God died for the Law which bears the
mark of the spirit so that its trace could be our mo-
tive to advance, our duty and goal.*

Above the desert, at the borders of what is writ-
ten, God becomes His look into the void.
O visage of the void where God sees Himself.)

Peace in our exile meant shadows piling up.

(Let this shadow be mine,
and I'll be a tree,
a fable of leaves.
Between me and the earth
nothing
but the pledge of sap.

The place where I wake up is the discovered
place.

"Death," said Yaël, "is a look abandoned by the
eyes.")

Forgive my book as I forgive yours.
Our nights are twins. We come from the same land.

PARALLEL EXISTENCE IV

All seeds have sprouted except one. Its fate is to
remain a seed.

Come closer, all my innumerable selves, and
talk, talk without stopping. Silence is torture, and I
am surrounded by silence.

I shall have been a Jew in the way a flower in the
desert is astonished by its own desires.

How can I be angry with those who deny my identity? The sand trusts only the sand.

Grain by grain, silence is restored to me.

Our days are twins, like facing pages of a book. We come from the country entrenched behind a universal Word. We did not know that we had unwittingly left it behind. In order to regain it we had to backtrack the roads of the exodus back to the destruction of the Temple—which is the ample Time around the breathless time that has become ours—as if it were from this destruction that the message went out of a people riveted to its displacement, that the message went out with all the broken stones of their dwelling.

Heap of stones. For centuries, God spoke through stone.

God spoke through the cracks in stones, and His people knew from then on that each of their wounds was in writing.

(I came and said: "I am absent from this brotherly absence among words. I am absent from these adjoining beaches which make words readable."

And you answered me: "Write your name after mine. Don't you know that freedom is in the sand knot of absence?"

From the middle of truth rises a light which we have kept intact. Glimmer of a secret word of both pity and pardon, sweet to the ear for having been kept at a distance, but also a word of distress like the root's scream smothered under the rock.

The middle of truth is a breach which no light bothers because day shines inside it and bristles against any admixture of strange light. So much does it want to be omnipotent.

Omnipotence, strange in itself, but unique. It makes the book.

The abyss will always break our freedom as it is
freedom in the nascent stage which is also the
ultimate.

In God, as in truth, we are chained.
We cannot conceive of liberty without life, yet it
is death which liberates us.

Freedom lies in the name we have earned as well
as in going beyond it. He who was nothing, the
naked being without ties or allies, will dissolve into
the universe, having already abrogated himself.

Memory, seasoned sap.

I dreamed of writing, and God was the sim-
plicity of my dream. I shall crumble with the wall,
struck dumb.

So simple, the death in God.
So simple, the life in God.)

The Jew cannot detach himself from his past. His present at its
best reflects the most beautiful days of old.

The Jew has always questioned the earth:
"Earth, earth, do you believe in me?"
The earth has never changed its response:
"I believe in those who claim me.
"I believe in those who disclaim me."

"I salute him,"
    said the earth,
"who loves me,"
    said the earth,

"who has unwittingly loved me,"
   said the earth,
"who came in the morning to surprise my sleep,"
   said the earth,
"who has watched time go by far from me,"
   said the earth,
"who in his heart rushed toward me,"
   said the earth,
"who chose me among all,"
   said the earth,
"who was not moved by his choice,"
   said the earth,
"who is tied to me by shed tears and blood,"
   said the earth,
"who bathed in his blood and his tears,"
   said the earth,
"who calmly paid the price of being Jewish,"
   said the earth,
"for whom I am a song,"
   said the earth,
"who is as old as the desert and rocks,"
   said the earth,
"who is as young as the poplars on my hills,"
   said the earth,
"whose memory is a fir,"
   said the earth,
"whose eyes carried my face off into death,"
   said the earth,
"whose will agrees with the prayer of the grain under stone,"
   said the earth,
"whose name is sweet like a lamp or dew,"
   said the earth,
"and all of you who are with him,"
   said the earth,
"and each of you in turn,"
   said the earth,
"I salute you."

The book is molded from clay.

> (*Here I stop.*
> *The threshold is both ground and sky.*
> *Here I put down the book*
> *and lie down heavy on each page*
> *in the night of my name.*
> *Here I am free and have no purpose*
> *but to vouch for the truth of a word*
> *whose judge and accomplice I am.*
> *If it gets light on the page*
> *the hour, a busy bee,*
> *will buzz around familiar syllables.*
> *If it is dark in the hollow of the book*
> *shadows dizzy with cutting loose from the night*
> *will gorge every letter with the black blood of*
> *their wounds*
> *and thus reveal its eternity to the days to come.*
> *Thus time is read*
> *from the beginning.*)

"I am only a word. Ah, how I need a face."
"I'll give you my face. I'll love it as if it were yours."

"Bitterness envelops the almond, prejudice of the gift."
"May the fruit be sweet."

Green, yellow, red: loud colors of our questions. The one which turns black is the abyss, the one which stays white, our obsession.

What you think you are is often what you want to be. Likewise the book.

Death lets us see the world as it was or will be.

Time is double where the track shows.

In what has been said, in what has returned to silence, there is our solitude.

For the Jew, having a place means finishing a book.
The unfinished book was our survival.

Sixth Approach to the Book

THE END AND THE MEANS

(To desire something passionately means suppressing the heat of any other desire, means fusing all your desires into one, possessing nothing in order to claim everything at once.

The most deprived have the maddest desires. Emptiness aspires to be filled.

Wanting to be the poorest for love in order to be one day—who knows?—the most fortunate.

Death turns away from our eyes all that henceforth can no longer call out to them and which, besides, irritates the void.)

In the quest I pursue there could not be any middle ground. The end is the means at my disposal for pushing back my limits through writing.

I constantly reach out as in calling or prayer. But I am not calling anybody, not praying.

The end is the impassable obstacle. What ruse could we use to be done with it—to be done with what is done?

Considering the end as means, is this not also giving the end the means to continue on into an after-the-end between two provisional ends in wait for future prolongations?

Spark, o desert of flight. Affidavit of the eye.

Can a call, a prayer bite through the silence around them? It would mean that ring and circle are the unlimited aspect of a limit closed on its adventure.

To keep within the sensible track, within a balance of life and death—of life in death and death in life—at the heart of the fateful question to God, namely, Where is the end?

THE CHOICE AND RIGHT TO WRITE

(To be read, to read yourself in death, is this what writing is?

In this case, the writer is, at the heart of the invisible, a captive reader of a translated universe which expresses him.

Could the knowledge we have of ourselves come from this reading?

You listen to yourself after stepping aside and again stepping aside for the unalienable page.

Between you and the earth, you have chosen the country which would have you in its image in which you can barely recognize yourself. But what matter since you will be the child of that exclusive part of the world with which you wanted one day to share your name.

"I shared my childhood name with the first cry of morning and have not had a name since.")

From one work to the next, the pursuit of an intransigent truth defines the road, pursuit without haste, however, and as if waiting for an encounter which would mark its arrival in (or prelude to) a regained totality.

Is truth a divine negation? Is the god of truth the God whose face we shall never see, but whose existence could be proved by one single clearing in the fogs of creation around Him? All that is exists only in terms of what it will not be. Thus God ruined Himself in the word to teach man how to die.

Being, things, the world have no other reality than that which destroys them. The time of truth is the ready wear and tear of time, the withering of the magnificent rose.

Beings and things unite and, insidiously, cancel each other out. Death is the source of eternity.

Judaism is perhaps, outside any interpretation, the singular idea that absence has it out with death at the moment we approach God, moment of a striking erasure among the circumscribed words, providential breach opening a passage for the book.

Could it be that my land exploded in a collision of the five continents? Where did I ever really set foot?

"My road was all ashes and ashes of ashes. The earth merged with my steps for so many years that it no longer seems the earth to me, but just one endless road," he said.

Maybe I too have walked so much that I have lost all sense of the earth and remember only my great tiredness and the sound of my steps.

And yet I took part in the struggles of men. I did not shirk choice.

Choice is the individual's liberation, his most fundamental right.

Who questions me returns me to the road.

Choice merges with maturity.

The book was my choice, later it became my right.

THE POWER OF KEYS

(*You who emerge from the core of the truth, who are distinguished by the core of the truth, who wear as a veil the litham of the core of the truth.*

"Stay at the core. Live at the core," said one of the sages of my books. "Because if God exists He is the core of soul and universe, the insatiable core of the core that cannot be.")

He asked: "I have lost time. I am always early or late. Am I on time today?"

"You are on time, no doubt," was the reply. "But which time are we on?"

In every work there is likely a key phrase, an image, some pages which we grasp only long after we saw them. As if this key had to shine in the night of the word so that we could use it only after having left the book.

Every trace is a key. The eyes do not resist emptiness. The night is escorted.

Ah, to emerge naked from the night and discover the morning we instinctively pursued. But sometimes the night ends within the night.

Will you read me where I no longer write?

I belong to that stubborn people that made a song out of its migrations and a book from its bedrock. But perhaps it had to stop walking one day to bury its pages.

> (*To find the track, almost transparent on the blank page, and to follow it. Thus a man lost in the desert follows any footprint, real or imagined, which might lead to an oasis. But it may happen that it leads through thirst and to death.*
>
> *My books are a multitude of tracks because I have walked the same paths over and over, because I got lost often. I have shuttled between hope and despair for so long that I do no longer know my age. My books are an echo of long anguish and a song of resurrection, an insistent appeal to life and a hymn to the glory of nudity regained.*

Facing the page, I am like a traveler without compass in the desert. No journey is mine. So that in chasing myself from one track to another I chase the journey. Tomorrow I shall leave as if I had always been on the point of departure.

This journey, forever put off, is nothing like an ordinary journey. It draws me into its wake without letting me know my destination. This journey, eternally prepared within the journey, is a migration across death, an innocent advance into the book until word separates from word silently to question itself. Transfer at the heart of a word which split in two in order to mirror itself in absence.

Double track of eternity, double mirage where the journey was never more than the moving and yet immobile place of the journey, the absurd attempt at winning where you must die.

Writing the book means, at this crucial stage of its course, writing existence in its most intimate silence. Death remains our first word.

From the chosen word to the forbidden word, from Sarah, girl broken by other people's hatred and who haunts the three panels of The Book of Questions, *to Yaël, saint and demon through the lie at the core of God's creation, then from Yaël to Elya, unbearable silence in a body of one single day, the pages of my books, to whose wound Yukel continues to testify, huddle close in face of the blinding truth. But what is a truth which does not straight off carry all votes? Mine can only be recognized by me, so much my own are its lacks and certainties.*

Elya knew nothing of writing, like those primitive tribes whose dreams fell silent with their voices. Nevertheless he remains the sign we have read in spite of him. So true is it that the book

*comes before the world which deciphers itself at its
peak; so true is it, Elya, that you were open to your
name before you were born to yourself in the
silence of an attentive page which you did not
disturb.*

*Endurance is a succession of miserable stones,
which are welcome for a rest, though, and on
which the words have shed some drops of blood.
Brown or red stains which the Jew recognizes because he remembers the wounds he suffered along
these same roads.*

*Man is a given, a find, and a reject. Every bor-
der flaunts its refusals.*

*I do not remember God. God thinks within the
creature. We are being thought even in our age-old
thoughts.*

*I offer what I probe and consider good. Evil is
malignant dark.*

*The ditch will never be a well, O blessing of the
void.*

*The heart loves and is loved only in the body, the
kindness of eyes.*

Truth, enemy of form, repudiates the heart.

God is lost in his dazzling nearness.)

THE POWER OF THOUGHT

*(The Jew is being thought in two ways. He is at
the center of two contradictory ways of thinking—
one exalts him in his absence, the other under-
mines his presence. Both of these he opposes to
what he claims is Jewish Thought, thought fortified
by the bankruptcy of the two other ways of thinking and for which he feels ready to die.*

*Way off, there is a thought which will soon
sweep away all others in order finally to take hold
of silence and the dream of words sleeping in rows.
God spoke through it
once and fell silent.*

*The power of thought depends on the complete
victory of sight.*

*May your thinking be innocent and in words of
innocence.
The Jew is naked in his knots and his night.)*

A glass globe, lit by a bulb inside, hangs from the ceiling of the room. It will go out on me in its turn. Then I will know that it allowed me to see at night.

Thought is alternately the glass globe and the electric bulb, the latter having its place inside the former.

If I paint the globe black I avenge the night. The bulb will doubt its light.

Expressing ourselves starts with a thought which, detached from us, leads us to an unknown place—a non-place?—where the words live.

The glass globe is this unknown place or non-place, the bulb the emigrant.

The book is woven into an elsewhere which leaves us out. It is the word already thought, but which rethinks itself while it is written down. We are invaded by words. Every one of them was a friend to me because I am a burned-out lamp which remembers its light and the world it lit up for a moment, but which it now sees only through its death.

Night is at the very gates of the book. At night, I received you, O vain, O sovereign thought, and surrendered my words.

We will have written in the night of the book, with the void for witness.

Seventh Approach to the Book

DEAD SPACE

The great dream of space exploration which our generation is living is, in the end, only the will to respond more confidently to the questions of origins, as if the latter expected from us a reply to what they are not.

Do the eyes have imagination? Certainly not, but how could you deny that they stimulate it?

We do not come back to the earth with arms, but disarmed.

The eyes are vaster than the look. What stops the latter is quickly left behind.

Without echo. With the careful, precise aim to awaken it.

The misery of light: that it lacks a corner of dark to rest in.

Out in space, between sycthe and scythe, to live a few seconds on oxygen reserves, with no air anywhere.

Moon without ivy.

The obstacle is not place, but the All ashamed to show itself in its ridiculous aspects where the Almost-Nothing bosses the world.

This time after time.

No face within the face, no place within the place. Our kingdom is the narrow passage between the half-glimpsed and the no-longer-seen.

Return to ashes. The constellations exchange promises. Time of respite. O night hatching flames. Water is the last tie to death, to the spring.

The word wears the scar of its death.

What the eyes seize is what death unveils little by little, and what we can only possess in dying.

The threshold is in the wake of thresholds, then in our uprooting.

To die—or desperate throw of dice. Chance mastered in its own verve.

We die by accident.

Death is on the far side of the sea where the sand is not cradled.

In the language of sand and wind God is a synonym for dune

. . . dune piled up, grain by grain, where the spirit blows across the desert.

Our relations with God are so difficult because we are always at the mercy of a grain of sand.

Let your hand full of sand tell the price of gold powder running out.

—You return the sand you have gathered to the sand in little hillocks. Your kind of homage to God.

(Was this all there was to the great adventure?
We knew that any place destined to be ours—no
matter how far off—is accepted failure. We had
decided to remain outside for a worthier failure.
No doubt this was unreasonable, but we had no
choice. We were trying to live in the gradual ascen-
dence of a day which reveals its dimension at the
heart of the real. Death is in sight, eternity in the
second look, the look of a grain of thirst or a dia-
mond longing for water.)

THE LOWER LIGHTS

"The eye is full of lamps," he said.
"Come down. The same lamps burn inside you."

You are outside the lamps at night, inside them
during the day.

(What are the words of the book but exiled
words with which the writer peoples his exile?
An outcast, you could only be understood and
eventually loved in and through the book.
But was the book not in turn stomped on by the
very people who had followed its paths?
Jewish solitude lies in the impossible outcome of
the book, like the world in a child's trapped look.
Blood bathed by the sky, blood heavy with pink
shadows.)

"Whoever comes has naked hands,"
he said.
"Whoever stays has his hands full,"
he said.
"Whoever stays is welcome."

> ("*Being Jewish means only this for me*," he said:
> "*to bear my exile as the camel bears its two humps*."
>
> "*Which characterizes the Jew: memory or for-
> getting?*"
> "*Both. Memory of suffering, forgetting of mis-
> fortune*.")

God remembers, and beings and things continue to exist.

Let your memory be your house, O my beloved.

I have been nothing but a stranger everywhere, and you, who
took my hand, but the lantern of my night and the chance of
morning.

Water carves out a career.
Salt is solitary.

It is always in relation to others that we assert ourselves.
To be yourself, methodically, in facing others; to know yourself,
try to be known, while facing the unknown in others.

I speak as a stranger to strangers, convinced that my brother is
among them.

"I will have spent my life looking in what exists for what does perhaps not exist," I said to him.

"And I mine," he replied, "reclaiming what I have vested in what disavows me."

The word forgets the person who wrote it.
This forgetting is the writ of its future.

Let my steps be a dance of words.

He said: "In front of the blank page I close my ears, I cover my eyes.
"God is terrible."

Before the One comes the dazzling void which we experience as the near advent of the One.

The Book Belongs Only to the Book

("*I have no blood but has been shed,*" he said,
"*no ink but has been claimed by the words among
which I ventured until, O transliteration of the
dark sign into letters of bone, I was only the beginning of a written death which the words let me
share.*

"*Invisible door. All houses are restored to the air.
Did you know that emptiness is a sequence of doors
lit by yesterday's light?*"

"*What is this place?*" he continued to note. "*A
nest at the bottom of which a bird has buried a
portion of eternity saved by its wings.*

"*Word, you were at least once a bird of prey, a
bird of night. Dawn found you dead. The page is
the implacable day.*")

THE BOOK

The dark has the light for its past, and light the dark.

Whichever path we take, the past sputters in the distance like the last bit of a wick.

We find the candle where we left it for the time of a reading.

The book is the place of these far-flung comings and goings

. . . from night to night, from this side of the past to the other.

The work I write immediately rewrites itself in the book.

This repeatability is part of its own breathing and of the reduplication of each of its signs.

If inspiration consists in filling your lungs with oxygen, expiration empties them of life, means gliding into the void.

Thus we only hold on to the world by agreeing, in advance, to die.

"The difficulty of writing," he said, "is only the difficulty of breathing in rhythm with the book."

"The book," he added, "is not a place, but a covert."

The word is dry at its death.

"Was it not a mouth propped open, round, which inspired the mathematicians to designate the void by a circle with an oblique bar?"

First Approach to Aely
(Breath)

Leave me suspended in my life where nothing turns solid.
Completion is the kiss of death.

Aely unfolds in time with silence spreading its wings.
He branches out beyond existence. Beyond you, Yaël. In Elya's
wake.

. . . His body, I thought, belongs to someone else, some other
night.

. . . Life without word or act, without wound or coupling, without listening or pardon.

To any life-beyond corresponds a death-beyond. This second life
and anachronistic death are sisters.

> (*Shadow of a child of shadows: Aely.*
> *And I said to myself that this shadow was per-*
> *haps always fused with that of Yaël cradling Elya*
> *in her arms and, later, with that of Elya with-*
> *out Yaël.*
> *Aely is the way death will escape me as life did.*
> *Elusive down to his name which we never know*
> *how to pronounce. He is what does not go out from*
> *or come to me. He is the apocalyptic void which*

*fascinates me from afar, which I can neither ap-
proach nor appreciate, which presents itself as the
very last moment of death, moment when a name
passes into its absence, which I will one day be
called to take on by no longer taking myself on.*

*Between these two deaths, at the heart of these
two deaths, breathes and no longer breathes the
world.*

*Hence there could be a dark among all dark, a
road among all roads, a line among all curved or
straight lines. And we do not even need to know it.
Behind us, above; before us, underneath: we shall
be spotted in our death by a death which nobody
could pay attention to and which will never ask
anything of us; a death which calls into question
everything down to the fundamental principle of
all existence, scoffing at it because we sense its in-
completeness, offering its own mystery instead; a
death which grabs our last chance to restore it to
itself as the dark gives the light back to the light;
a death forgotten by death, insensitive to either
idea or form and ruling a smooth universe. Then
nothing has any sense. The question "Who are we?"
is superfluous. Nothing concerns us any more,
nothing, nothing, nothing . . .)*

It is in the vague space of an anticipated word that Aely would
watch us.

Who could have foreseen that silence is so patient? O night.

The world leaves us in peace unless we indulge in confidences.

There is that which finishes us off and then finishes off what, even
finished, still contains a particle of us.

There is a finish coincident with any finishing, but which resists it
in order to finish it off in its future.

Aely, power of the farthest distance

. . . power of farthest distance and of what has not been thought.
Could it be that the void resets our name backwards?
Listen to time breathing. Eternity's breath is imperceptible.

Second Approach to Aely
(The Street)

Abiding word, posted as if on sentry duty. You
defy me. Guard of which palace, which prison?
Of which night before night? Of which day before days?
Of which cherished presence? Of which regret-
ted absence?
—Guard of death, perhaps?

In the book which borrowed his name, Elya
claims a body, and, near him, Yaël finds hers.
Aely doubly loses his body here. Forgetting Yaël
means also forgetting death.

Zachary marches, seems in a hurry.
Yves dawdles.
Xavier purrs sweet nothings into Wilfrede's ear who swoons with
delight.
Victor follows pensively.
Uriel runs into another pedestrian and accuses him of not
watching out.
Theresa bends down to pick up a fashion magazine she had
dropped.
Simon meditates for a moment in front of a poster, then disap-
pears into a bistro.
Raoul gets out of his car and enters the hospital where his pa-
tients are waiting.
Quentin photographs a dead end.

Paulette, sheathed in a short silk dress, lets eyes take it off her without blushing.

Oliver and Norbert hail each other across the street. They will meet later in the Science Building of Winehall.

Moses suddenly shivers. He turns the collar of his raincoat up. The sky is grey. Is it going to rain?

Leopoldine comes back from the market with full bags.

Kui-Yuan goes down rue Pestalozzi, perhaps attracted by one of the two Chinese restaurants there.

Ismael, Hussein, and Gabr argue, gesticulate, scream, howl with laughter.

Felicien slowly passes on his bicycle.

Elie does not have long to live. He is helped across the street.

Denise has run into Camille and Bernadette. She invites them up to the attic room she has just rented across from the little Théâtre de l'Epée-de-Bois.

Adrien is embarrassed and humbly admits to some young Scandinavian women that he does not know this part of town. They asked him for the rue des Patriarches which, O irony, is right in front of them.

Abraham-Adam looks out his window.

It is raining on this June morning.

Alphabet book, as old as its worn letters and different inks, I see my name disintegrate and reform in it any moment.

Without a body man's life span could be centuries.

The end of things will not be the end or beginning or rebeginning of the end, but oblivion. It comes before and after death. Oblivion of the end. Oblivion of the beginning.

My street is prodigious in that it partakes of all the streets in the world. Yet it is short and narrow. The building in its middle houses the post office. There it suffers a change which opens it to the five continents. In the form of stamps, with every letter, every postcard, every package to other countries, cities, villages, it goes out to meet its memories, becomes other streets. Thus it is always elsewhere.

Here, it joins two streets which otherwise would not have known each other.

Third Approach to Aely
(The Dream)

Eye in the perplexity and keenness of the eye.

Who will follow it, this dream of the first con-
tagious sleep of the book?
It barely grazed the word which had enriched
the day.

I was walking. The road: ink, limpid, nearly blue. Looking up—
or was I looking down?—I felt reassured as by a friendly presence
whose hand I could see clutching a pen. It diligently copied my
name in slanted letters. But it did not look like any other hand and
perhaps was none. It made me think of a young octopus. No doubt
because we had touched the bottom of the ocean. Do not aquatic
animals in dying or delirious liberty take the sky for the unreachable
bottom of the water?
"Aely," I murmured, "child, void, monster, shadow, hand, let me
see you."
And a voice in the void repeated: "Let me see you," distinctly repeated: "Let me see you," as if speaking to a father, a brother, a son.

> (*"Only death remembers all the faces that are
> gone today.*
> *"We enter eternity thanks to death's memory."*)

What if, for the universe, the earth were a final eye? It would confirm our planet as the final period in the Book of God. Then writing would be forbidden to us. The book would remain unappeased desire of the book, longing for the refused words.

Aely, brother, father, son of rebellion: father, brother, son of what is written.

The eye is a lock for any key.

> ("*The dream above the stagnant waters of murder,*" he said, "*is a silence whose lapsed images the eye intercepts.*
>
> "*Like old ladies glued behind curtains by their curiosity we watch the word through the many crevices of death, as if suddenly light had become too painful.*
>
> "*Never have our heels crushed the fat silt of the river bank.*
>
> "*So green a vise! Yet it let us drift down to the sea.*")

What if, for the earth, God were the final eye?
What if, for God, man were in the end the final eye?

Fourth Approach to Aely
(The Sign)

The word always faces the unknown.

Proof has no power.

Here, the bond is perhaps the sign. But no bond
troubles the letter.
Aely, sign under the sign.

"God," he said, "preserves the distance from
One to One."

It is through signs that Aely compelled recognition. While reading certain books I was suddenly strangled by an anxiety whose
cause I could not pin down. It was as if I were in the presence of
my death.

I was far from suspecting that my book had reached that ridge in
the middle of emptiness where no plant grows and all birds flee.
Imagine my surprise to find an alphabet there traced in stone.

But how could this isolated peak hold up in space? With every
word, the infinite explodes the boundaries of the book. The writer
lives in an atmosphere of letters ground fine. The air he breathes is
heavy with the dust of words he puts his wits to recreating. Ill wind
fills his lungs.

The strange peak is nothing but a mad pile of figures, of letters
caught and milled by space and petrified by centuries.

A reading of emptiness could only be undertaken on the scale of a
disintegrated world. From our expeditions into the abyss we bring

back a book reshaped by death and which fits our hands. O same-
ness of letter and figure in the heart of the final sign.

"The One is the speculative absence of the One," he said.

"Any figure is the All, the less or the more.

"Any letter is the All, the distance and knot.

"The less is untouched distance, the more is the knot. For example: the more milestones on the road, the more knots in our
wandering."

The universe is a figure before it is a word. O revival of the book.

"Writing," he said, "is perhaps only bearing witness, with the help
of the pen, to the inevitable encounter of word and figure, fire and
fire, river and sea."

. . . Figure within indefinite figures, word within the devouring
solitude of the book.

To become an indistinguishable part of the omnipresent totality
by doing away with limits.

Absence. Absences.

     (*"I value words for their infinite effacement and
daily resonance. Thus I humbly have to make al-
lowance for myself," he said, "but only as for a tree
which has serenely let drop its leaves."*

     *"The only word which can, in a pinch, rival the
word 'death,'" he said elsewhere, "is the word 'universe.' But what could you oppose to the word
'void'? Perhaps the word with which it shares two
letters: 'God.'*

     "Thus we can bear our nothingness."

     *The void inside a circle, Aely's eye, eye of death.
Have I done nothing with the words of mystery but
turn unflaggingly around an eye, a mirror?*

     *"It is obvious," he said again, "that the word
mort, 'death,' and the word univers, 'universe,' are
bound together by the letter 'r' which otherwise
opposes them.*

"R *for* RESPIRATION.
The air of the universe is the air death takes from our lungs.

So dying is a last, painful sigh which gives the universe back to the universe, that is, gives back to the void all the space death entrusted to death.

Then the void is nothing but life emptied of being, and its call perhaps a desperate call back to life.

One word will cross the whole book without hindrance. This word is soif, *'thirst,' brother of salt and sand and also, at its inescapable end, dried-up brother of silence.*

We have seen our own names undone one after another. Likewise undone, from border to border, the names of Sarah, Yukel, Yaël, Elya, and Aely.

The word soif, *'thirst,' will have the same fate in turn.*

Because the divine Name wanted its surface legibility to be unpronounceable, any word is fatally destined to anonymous absence.

I have watched fall and, falling, come apart the letter "s," then the three others. Then I thought I could read in the mirror of the void, where they had in passing looked at themselves, the word foi.

Foi, *faith in the book. Faith in the letter.*

The plural of a word is formed by adding an "s," grammar teaches the schoolchild, plunging him into the heart of miracle.

O Queen of past and future identity, of radiant repetition and irrepressible becoming in death.

Thirst. Sand. Salt.

O silence, deaf horizon.

God is the unquenched desire of the letter.)

The Star

You will leave this book by the light of the first and last star. We have never known the day. And yet, which day did we fail to invoke in our supplications? If it is true that every color which dazzles us is black inside—"the eighth color is black. It is inside all colors, their blood, their nourishing night"—if it is true that the perilous passage through the tunnel we were induced to undertake means that we have been worming our way through the depth of the book, crawling most of the time and waking up rolled around ourselves, then the star which is at the beginning and end is our salvation. Star which shows that the book was completed before it was begun. Star of mathematicians, glittering with all the possible functions of the mind, but not all its openings. Star also which Sarah and Yukel had worn on their chests and later, denizens of a different sky, hung up on the firmament of our ineffable grief.

The law bestraddles this same star. The law is not given, but revealed to us by each word as we progress in the book, word by word in the melodious oblivion of words. O music of death.

. . . But what if writing were, paradoxically, the need to shield the word against the attraction of the mythic book? Need which the writer gladly obeys to save himself from despair?

O flight in the mire,

headlong return to the Void.

The other side of a letter is, then, this side of any night.

"Does writing not mean," he said, "without respite delivering the word from the hold of the next word so that we may find intact, though secretely bruised, the white page, the page of eternity?"

Alain's Letter

Monsieur,

I am leaving. I am coming clear. Have I forced you to take up your pen again? You have been writing on my silence. I am breaking this silence. I am breaking with my dead-life. Elya, whose name and then book I have taken on myself, will now be the song of my night. I shall listen to him often, as seriously as I listened to you these two years. So many misunderstandings lie in wait for your works. But is this an evil? The evil is within you, Monsieur. It is inherent in writing, and I have been its image. How could I bear this fate any longer and not die? But was it not a dead man my mother dragged to you so you should give him back life, that is, words, your words? I claimed them only so that you could survive, as Yaël in her madness lived off Elya. Because we were both damned. I was somehow the pretext for a book through which all your books expected a sign from you, perhaps the final one. This book is on your table. It remained between us while I stayed. Now it is between you and *the others*, between you and the day. What matter if the morning will not see us together. I am bound to leave you. Innocence is the daughter of oblivion. Knowledge the stammering of a providential birth. I am going to be born. Are you going to be cured?

(Aely, from which world where you have not lived have you inherited this absent look of the hangman, the executioner?

The book is the price of parting.

*Perhaps writing means revealing the word to
yourself at death's threshold.)*

Will my work—as you, Yaël, called the heavy, broken chain of
my writings—will my work hold up among the innumerable and
contradictory definitions of God, and my solitude, in the death of
this word?

O undefinable universe. O book without offspring, whose words
are only deferred waiting for words.

Can what is black through God remain black without God? And
what is white?—What is white never lets go of its whiteness, which
is both hope and despair of white, the fore- and after-birth of day.

Then being Jewish means following God on the road of whiteness
and turning what seems a divine trace into a letter worn away as
soon as it appears.

God's clothing: a white shroud.
The Jew refuses the shroud.

I shall not answer Alain.

*(The book is destroyed by the book. We shall
never have owned anything.)*